CW00541100

THE REVIVAL
A Ghost Play

James Cawood was born in Newcastle upon Tyne and trained as an actor at the Bristol Old Vic Theatre School.

Between 2004 and 2010 James worked across Theatre, Film and TV as an actor in the UK and Europe. In 2007 James wrote his first play *The Jeffersons* which received a rehearsed reading at the Bristol Old Vic Studio. His second play, *Farmhands* (2008) was shortlisted for the International Playwriting Award and his play *A Mooncalf Tattoo* (2009) was Longlisted for the Verity Bargate Award at the Soho Theatre. Whilst working as an actor at Vienna's English Theatre he was challenged to write a thriller for their upcoming season; the result was *Stone Cold Murder*. After receiving its World Premiere in Vienna in 2011, *Stone Cold Murder* has gone on to enjoy a very successful UK Tour and has been produced across Europe as well as in New Zealand and Australia. The play has subsequently been translated into German under the title *Ein Brillanter Mord* and received its German Language Premiere in 2014 and has embarked upon a nationwide German tour.

His follow up thriller, *Death Knell* received its world premiere at Theatre Royal, Windsor before a nationwide UK Tour. It has subsequently been produced across Europe.

He lives in the Cotswolds with his wife, Olivia.

THE REVIVAL
A Ghost Play

by James Cawood

JOSEF WEINBERGER PLAYS

LONDON

THE REVIVAL – A Ghost Play
First published in 2018
by Josef Weinberger Ltd
12-14 Mortimer Street, London W1T 3JJ
www.josef-weinberger.com / plays@jwmail.co.uk

Copyright © 2018 by James Cawood
Copyright © 2015 by James Cawood as an unpublished dramatic composition

The author asserts his moral right to be identified as the author of the work.

ISBN: 978 0 85676 374 8

This play is protected by Copyright. According to Copyright Law, no public performance or reading of a protected play or part of that play may be given without prior authorization from Josef Weinberger Plays, as agent for the Copyright Owners.

From time to time it is necessary to restrict or even withdraw the rights of certain plays. It is therefore essential to check with us before making a commitment to produce a play.

NO PERFORMANCE MAY BE GIVEN WITHOUT A LICENCE

AMATEUR PRODUCTIONS
Royalties are due at least one calendar month prior to the first performance. A royalty quotation will be issued upon receipt of the following details:

Name of Licensee
Play Title
Place of Performance
Dates and Number of Performances
Audience Capacity and ticket price(s)

PROFESSIONAL PRODUCTIONS
All enquiries regarding professional rights should be addressed to Josef Weinberger Plays at the address above.

OVERSEAS PRODUCTIONS
Applications for productions overseas should be made to our local authorised agents. Further information can be found on our website or in our printed Catalogue of Plays.

CONDITIONS OF SALE
This book is sold subject to the condition that it shall not by way of trade or otherwise be re-sold, hired out, circulated or distributed without prior consent of the Publisher. **Reproduction of the text either in whole or part and by any means is strictly forbidden.**

This book has been typeset in sans-serif fonts to assist with accessibility for visually impaired readers.

Printed by Edward Dudfield Ltd.

To Judy

My mother-in-law

A connoisseur of the ghost story

THE REVIVAL – A Ghost Play was first presented at the Sheringham Little Theatre, Norfolk on 11th August 2017. The cast was as follows (in order of appearance):

MICHAEL PRENTICE
Tim Welton

HUGO TILLING-HUNT (TIMOTHY GREY)
Jack Finch

ALISON WOODLEY (PENELOPE MAKEPEACE)
Lesley Anne Acheson

DIANA SOUTH (ZELMA VAN TANZEN)
Lynn Whitehead

EDDIE WILDE (GERALD MAKEPEACE)
Steve Banks

SOPHIE ESSENHEIMER (BETSY GREY)
Rachel Smyth

GILES HEATH
Tim Freeman

CLIVE MUNRO
Harry Williams

Directed by Gillian King

Set and Lighting Design by Matthew Coomber

CHARACTERS

THE DIRECTOR

Michael Prentice
Late 40's. A theatre director who has enjoyed varying degrees of success. Slightly theatrical but not to the point of cliché.

THE ACTORS

Sophie Essenheimer (Betsy Grey)
20's. Very pretty. Shy and unassuming although she knows how attractive she is. American.

Hugo Tilling-Hunt (Timothy Grey)
Early 30's. A public school educated, handsome young man with the confidence and brio that comes with such a background.

Diana South (Zelma Van Tanzen)
60's. An actress who has seen it all, regarded as the consummate, if occasionally jaded, professional.

Eddie Wilde (Gerald Makepeace)
Late 30's to 40's. An actor who will, in the coming years, be described as a 'character actor.'

Alison Woodley (Penelope Makepeace)
Late 30's. The dependable actress who has worked with Michael a number of times and can be relied upon to do a job.

STAGE MANAGEMENT

Clive Munro
Anything from 20's to 40's. A stage manager.

and . . .

Giles Heath
60's.

SETTING

The action takes place in the present – ostensibly in the theatre in which it is being performed.

The stage is dressed and designed for a revival of the 1946 classic ghost play, *'Scared to Death'* by Lucian O'Keefe, the stage directions for which are below.

> *The entrance / living room of an elegant Victorian house in the English countryside; comfortable though remote. Heavily furnished and dimly lit. A good drive in a motorcar from the nearest town.*

The set is almost finished though there are suggestions that finishing touches are required i.e. paint pots, a stepladder, etc.

> *On the back wall, centre stage is a heavy double front door, slightly raised on a step. On either side of this door are two large sash windows looking out over a large driveway and lawn. Window seats beneath the windows.*

(The SR window is currently open.)

> *In the USL corner a door that leads into the dining room.*

> *Centrally located on the SL wall is a large fireplace with a heavy mantelpiece and surround. The fire spits and crackles as if a log has been recently placed on the flames.*

(Although currently this is not the case.)

> *SR a staircase leading up to bedrooms.*

> *Centre SR a further door leading into the library.*

> *Further decorations include a drinks table, adorned by full bottles of Scotch, gin and bitters.*

(These may be prop bottles currently– inelegantly labelled by stage management to inform the actors which liquor they are meant to include.)

A bookcase built into the wall with a fine array of books bound in rich colours.

Romantic landscape paintings by lesser known artists.

A large settee and two comfortable easy chairs.

Wall-mounted electric lights.

A gramophone.

A rug from the Orient centre stage.

This is a house decorated in a classic and British way and doesn't in any way bow to the modern fancy for the minimalist or 'art deco' style so prevalent in today's interior design. Indeed, it may seem dusty, anachronistic even for a contemporary audience – certainly for the younger generation for whom such weighty and, dare I say, oppressive furnishings are anathema.

ACT ONE

As the curtain rises we see TIMOTHY GREY, *a young man in his early thirties dressed formally for dinner, pouring himself a large measure of whisky and placing the needle down on the gramophone – modern jazz plays loudly and obnoxiously as he sits down, closes his eyes and takes a sip from his glass . . .*

[This does not happen. In fact we see no action. The stage is quiet and the lights on stage are dimmed to the point of near darkness. Silence – for as long as is feasible.]

The SR sash window slams shut with a crash. MICHAEL PRENTICE *rushes onto the stage, fumbling in the darkness.*

MICHAEL   Clive! Clive! Lights up!

                 (*Nothing.*)

                 Clive?!

                 (*He waves his arms madly whilst looking up to the 'box'.*)

                 For God's sake, Clive bring up the bloody lights!

                 (*The house lights and stage lights snap on almost violently.* MICHAEL *shields his eyes from the shock of the glare.*)

                 Thank you.

                 (MICHAEL *walks over the window and inspects it.*)

                 (*Back to* CLIVE.) Make a note – another bloody note . . . to have this looked at. And I know what you're going to say, Clive, so don't say it. I know what's coming . . . (*Mocking.*) "But Michael we want it to slam shut". Yes, we do. But we want it to slam shut on cue! Not when the tired, stressed and frankly on-the-edge-of-

a-nervous-breakdown director is trying to have
five minutes' shut eye backstage! (*Mumbling and
going back to the window.*) Gave me a bloody
heart attack.

(*Beat.*)

Clive? Can you even hear me? CLIVE! If you can
hear me . . . dim the lights.

(*The lights dim and come back up.*)

Thank you. And you've made a note of the
window?

(*Lights dim and come back up.*)

Good. And do you appreciate that if this
window slams shut again at any time other than
when dictated by the script, you will be sacked
on the spot?

(*Lights dim and come back up very, very
slowly.*)

Very funny, Clive. Now stand by . . . we may as
well run through the sound cues whilst we're
waiting for the others to get back.

(MICHAEL *goes back to the window and opens
it again. He struggles for a second and just as
he manages to open the window* HUGO TILLING-
HUNT *jumps out from the other side with a
roar.* MICHAEL *falls over with shock and* HUGO,
*casually sitting on the window ledge, finds this
very funny.*)

HUGO	(*Not very.*) Sorry, Michael! I do apologise.
MICHAEL	What the bloody hell do you think you're doing?

HUGO	(*Coming through the window.*) Well, it's in keeping, don't you think . . . With the whole . . . Just building a little atmosphere. God knows we need it.
MICHAEL	What was that?
HUGO	Nothing. I don't think I said anything.
MICHAEL	Listen, you want atmosphere – you build it! You're the actors, not me. My job is almost done but yours has only just started.
HUGO	(*Mouths the last sentence with rolling eyes.*) I know, I know. Michael . . . Michael. Micky boy.
MICHAEL	Don't call me that.
HUGO	You're wonderful. You really are. We all know that. And you and me. Me and you. How many times have we worked together now?
MICHAEL	Must be getting on for . . .
HUGO	Eleven times. Eleven. Christ! There are showbiz marriages built on less that that.
MICHAEL	If that's a proposal . . . ?
HUGO	All I am saying, the real truth of what I am saying . . . is that we, your players, we know how good you are. We know how good dear Clive is up in his cosy little box. And we know how good we are . . . we know each other's talent and potential, yes?
MICHAEL	(*Unsure of where this is going.*) Y-e-s?
HUGO	So there can't be an issue there.
MICHAEL	Where?

HUGO	There. Where we know. Each other. One another.
MICHAEL	Listen, Hugo, dear . . . I appreciate this . . . I really do, but I have to admit I have absolutely no idea what you're talking about.
HUGO	We are the links, yes? We know the links. Me, Eddie, Alison and dear old Diana . . .
MICHAEL	Don't let her hear you call her that.
HUGO	We all know one another. We all know what it's like to be under pressure the night before we open. And we know what we're capable of. And we're capable of brilliance.
MICHAEL	Then please feel free to show it.
HUGO	We will . . . we are, Michael. Christ! You know Diana turned down the RSC for this?
MICHAEL	I hardly need reminding.
HUGO	What I am saying is . . . that we are strong links. Welded together by years in the industry. But we can only be . . . well . . . as strong as our weakest link.
MICHAEL	Ah, I see. How very predictable . . .
HUGO	No, now listen . . .
MICHAEL	I see what you're doing.
HUGO	I'm not making excuses.
MICHAEL	Well, it certainly sounds like that. This conversation is over.
HUGO	Oh, come on, Michael! You know as well as I do this had to come out. We have to address the elephant in the room.

MICHAEL	Enough! I have less than twenty-four hours to get this play into some kind of shape and for that I need you, all of us, to pull together. And here you are causing rifts. Blaming those who aren't here to defend themselves.
HUGO	Then you defend her! Go on. You hired her.
MICHAEL	So you're blaming me?!
HUGO	The buck's got to stop somewhere.
MICHAEL	How dare you!
HUGO	It's only because I love you, Michael. And your work. I know what you're capable of making this play. And that is a huge, smash hit. I know it. I feel it. I am safe in your hands. But you've got to admit . . .
MICHAEL	No, no. That's quite enough. Go and get ready and this is the last I want to hear about it. Back on stage in five minutes. I'm off to check sales with box office. And when I return I will have forgotten all about this . . . manipulative and frankly bitchy conversation.
	(MICHAEL *begins to descend the stairs into the auditorium leaving* HUGO *alone on stage.*
	Pause.
	HUGO *shouts after him . . .*)
HUGO	All we want you to do is admit that she's bloody awful and she's dragging us all down with her!
MICHAEL	(*Spinning around.*) And what do you want me to do? Huh? Sack her the night before we open?
HUGO	That's not unheard of. We're only previewing! These things happen all the time. I mean, no

offence to this play you have carefully chosen
to revive . . . but she's hardly playing Hedda
bloody Gabler . . . there are hundreds of girls
we could rehearse in in a few days and would
be up to speed and better than her by the time
we opened.

MICHAEL   (*Walking away again, dismissively.*) Impossible
               and impractical! Go and get ready!

HUGO   (*With a hint of venom.*) We've all guessed,
               Michael. We can see it from a mile off.

               (MICHAEL *stops dead in his tracks.*)

               You're screwing her. Aren't you?

               (MICHAEL *begins to walk back towards the stage.*)

MICHAEL   If you don't want this to be last time we work
               together, and by that I mean the last time you
               ever work at all, I suggest you desist from this
               line of enquiry immediately.

HUGO   (*Sitting down on one of the chairs.*) I only ask . . .
               man to man . . . as she may be quite incapable
               of remembering lines and simply dreadful at any
               form of acting at all but what I would say is that
               her major redeeming feature is that she is quite
               simply one of the sexiest little things I have ever
               had the pleasure to meet.

MICHAEL   Now listen . . .

HUGO   So I just want to ask . . . how did you bag that?
               You saucy bastard.

MICHAEL   You're going too far now, Hugo!

HUGO   Unless. Yes . . . of course. That's how she got
               the job! And I thought the casting couch was a
               thing of the past.

MICHAEL   (*Leaping up the stairs and going for him.*) Now listen here you jumped-up little shit . . .

                 (*Enter* ALISON WOODLEY. *She is in costume and holds an envelope.*)

ALISON   Evening! Oh, I'm sorry . . . are you running lines? I thought we were called for the top of Act One?

MICHAEL   (*Composing himself.*) Alison, darling. You were. Thank God one of you knows what's going on.

HUGO   Oh, I know what's going on all right.

ALISON   Sorry?

HUGO   (*Getting up and going to kiss* ALISON *on each cheek.*) Nothing. You look fabulous in that. Simply fabulous.

ALISON   Thank you.

HUGO   You went to that vegetarian place for dinner, didn't you? Any good?

ALISON   Well I thought it was wonderful.

HUGO   Ah.

ALISON   Diana I think was less enamoured.

HUGO   Oh God, did she misbehave?

DIANA   (*Off.*) Was I meant to receive a call in my dressing room? Bloody amateur hour. Clive? Clive?

                 (*Enter* DIANA *in her rather elaborate costume carrying a newspaper. She sweeps in centre stage and looks straight up to the box.*)

DIANA   Clive? Was I meant to receive a call in my
               dressing room? (*To the others.*) Is he up there?

MICHAEL   As much as Clive can be anywhere.

DIANA   Clive, darling. We all know you and love you.
               And we forgive your little . . . foibles . . . but
               if you neglect to give me a call to my dressing
               room again I assure you, these seemingly
               withered arms shall bely their weakened state
               and shall string you up by your puny little balls
               . . . you understand?! Clive?!

MICHAEL   (*Putting his arm around her and leading her
               away.*) I'm sure he does, Diana my love. He's
               under pressure, just like the rest of us.

DIANA   I really don't know why you insist on employing
               him.

MICHAEL   Call it misguided loyalty.

DIANA   Pah! I call it cheap. Pay peanuts, get monkeys,
               that's what I say.

MICHAEL   Perhaps, but we've got to turn a profit.

HUGO   (*Kissing* DIANA *on both cheeks.*) And he's got
               your astronomical wages to worry about.

DIANA   And quite right too. I could have been in
               Stratford right now. (*Towards the box.*) Getting
               calls in my dressing room!

HUGO   But you wouldn't be having as much fun.

DIANA   You know they wanted me to play The Witch of
               Edmonton?

MICHAEL   And now you're very successfully playing
               The Witch of [*Insert name of current town /
               theatre.*] . . .

DIANA	Very funny, Michael. Very droll. But may I remind you I am quite capable of running out of this little vanity project of yours at any time I like so I suggest you make sure I receive calls in my dressing room from now on. Yes?
MICHAEL	I assure you, once we're under way, you'll all be getting calls to your dressing rooms. We just need to iron out the teething problems.
DIANA	Yes, that's a point . . . where is she?
ALISON	Don't, Diana. That's very mean. She's got a difficult part. Lots of lines.
DIANA	Difficult part? Hardly. The Witch of Edmonton, now *that's* a difficult part. Her part is all teeth and tits. Wouldn't you agree, Michael?
MICHAEL	(*Inspecting the set.*) Mmm?
DIANA	(*Sharing this with* HUGO.) You of all people should know how good she is at that.
MICHAEL	I'm going to check in with box office.
	(MICHAEL *descends into the auditorium and leaves during the following . . .*)
ALISON	Now stop it. Just because you're in a bad mood about the restaurant.
DIANA	(*Now reading her paper.*) What? The hummus hostel you insisted on taking me to for dinner. You can hardly call that a restaurant. Disgraceful.
HUGO	Not your idea of fine dining?
DIANA	I am of an age where I need iron and plenty of it. Iron and wine. And this one decides to take me for dinner at a place that balks at the mere

	mention of a steak and the only wine they had was low alcohol organic Greek muck!

ALISON   It's won awards, actually.

DIANA   So have I! Two Oliviers and a Tony! But if you came to my house for dinner you'd get a good steak and a bottle of Bordeaux. I'm sorry, Alison my dear . . . it was very kind of you to treat me to dinner this evening but I don't care how many hippy awards you win or how much sauce you try and drown your dishes in, a chickpea is a chickpea is a chickpea. And a chickpea does not a tasty meal make.

ALISON   (*Evidently quite hurt.*) Well I liked it.

           (*A heavy knocking at the front door.*)

DIANA   Enter, only if you wish to celebrate mediocrity!

           (*Enter* EDDIE, *dressed in dinner jacket and bow tie . . . this is of course his costume.*)

EDDIE   Why change the habit of a lifetime? Hello folks? All set for fear and murder and the dark arts?

DIANA   Tell me, darling. How do you maintain such a positive, sunny disposition when all around you is grey, dull and frankly cursed?

EDDIE   (*Looking around.*) Oh . . . that's a point where is she?

HUGO   One hopes she's had the decency to run away and never come back.

EDDIE   Now that would be a shame.

HUGO   Eddie, buddy. I speak for everyone when I say we appreciate all your efforts . . . we really do. Relentless. That's the word. Relentless. But . . .

and I mean this in the kindest possible way . . .
you don't have a chance. She's taken. She's off
the menu. No cards you can play will win that
fair maiden.

EDDIE   I take your challenge and I accept.

ALISON   God, it's pathetic.

HUGO   We've talked about this . . . she's screwing
               Michael. We all know it.

EDDIE   Which means she has very low standards.

DIANA   And it also means she knows where her bread
               is buttered. And you, Eddie my love, are neither
               bread, butter nor knife. You are, most likely,
               hummus.

EDDIE   What the hell does that mean?

ALISON   Ignore her.

EDDIE   (*To* HUGO.) Hadn't you better get into costume?
               I thought we were running Act One.

HUGO   Guess so. (*Up to box.*) Clive?! Shout me when
               our leading lady arrives will you? I could do
               with a laugh.

               (*He exits.*)

EDDIE   What have you got there?

ALISON   It's for Michael. It was in his pigeonhole. Must
               have missed it.

EDDIE   Probably the bank asking for their money back.

ALISON   I don't see why you're all so negative. This is
               an exciting opportunity. Unique. We are in the
               very fortunate position of reviving a lost classic

and you lot are shutting us down before we've
even opened.

DIANA   In my experience there's often a reason why
               lost classics have been lost.

ALISON   Then tell me, why did you accept the job?

DIANA   Go into my dressing room. Top drawer. In
               there you will find my contract. About two
               thirds down you'll see a section headed
               'remuneration'. The numbers following the
               pound sign. That's the reason.

ALISON   You weren't excited by the prospect of a
               possible West End transfer of *Scared to Death*
               by Lucien O'Keefe.

DIANA   Were you?

ALISON   Of course.

DIANA   Balls! No you weren't. And I'll tell you why . . .
               because you'd never heard of it! Nobody has.
               You, like the rest of us in this industry just want
               to be wanted. You said yes to the job because
               otherwise you'd be temping in some office on
               Old Street and cringing every time someone
               approached you at the photocopier and asked if
               you'd ever done any telly. Am I right?

EDDIE   Spot on.

ALISON   Well I must say I am disappointed. I would have
               thought out of all of us you would be the one to
               drive it towards success.

DIANA   Listen, I am more than happy to drive this
               production wherever it is meant to go but
               unfortunately we have a passenger on board
               who is determined to make us crash!

ALISON	You can't blame her for everything. We are an ensemble.
DIANA	Exactly. And we all therefore have to pull our weight. Tell me, are you off book?
ALISON	Of course, you know I am.
DIANA	And you remember all your blocking?
ALISON	Yes.
DIANA	And you have found your character and are now looking forward to flying with this play and enjoying the process of performance.
ALISON	I don't know what you're getting at.
DIANA	What I am getting at is that that is the minimum required of a professional. That's what we all have to do as an ensemble. But if just one of us neglects even one part of any of those processes, we're fucked. Yes? And that little American tart may have tits to die for and legs that could support Tower Bridge . . . but she's sure as dammit not an actress. And we're all going to go down together.
ALISON	Well, maybe we should help her.
EDDIE	We've tried. We've all tried.
DIANA	Some harder than others.
EDDIE	That's not fair. It's not all about trying to get her into bed.
DIANA	No. I'm sure you'd be happy to do it anywhere. The point is, Alison dearest, you can't polish a turd. And tomorrow night we're beginning previews on a great big, stinking turd.

ALISON	Well, you never know. We could be selling out.
EDDIE	Oh, we're selling out all right.
ALISON	I want this be a success and I don't believe you lot do. What's to say we don't have six months advanced bookings . . . in which case we'll just have to get on with it and be a smash hit!
MICHAEL	(*Bursting through from the foyer into the auditorium.*) FUCK IT! Twelve per cent! Twelve . . . can you believe it? We have sold twelve per cent of our tickets for the entire run!
DIANA	What's that noise? Oh, that's it. It's Alison's naïve positivity crumbling all around her.
MICHAEL	(*Making his way onto the stage.*) I can't breathe. I think my heart is stopping. I am seeing spots in front of my eyes.
ALISON	(*Rushing over to help him into a chair.*) Come on . . . sit down. It'll be fine. We haven't even previewed. We haven't even had press night. That'll change everything. Trust me. I can feel it.
MICHAEL	Twelve per cent!
ALISON	Is better than none.

(MICHAEL *throws her a look.*)

Well it is! Come on, sweetie. We have to trust in our abilities. Think positively. Eddie?

EDDIE	Well, you know me. Always the one with a sunny disposition.
ALISON	Exactly.
EDDIE	But twelve per cent . . .

ALISON   Eddie!

EDDIE   I'm just saying.

MICHAEL   You know I re mortgaged my house for this. A
                revival of *Scared to Death* by Lucian O'Keefe.
                Here, in the very theatre it was originally
                produced in. It had success written all over it.
                A few months here, maybe a tour and then into
                the West End. I could see it. Really see it.

ALISON   And you still can. I believe in it. I really do. It's
                going to be a huge success. But not if you mope
                and get depressed. We have to rehearse. Get
                the wheels turning once again. And the rest will
                take care of itself. Trust me. Michael . . . look at
                me.

                (*He does.*)

                We're going to be fabulous.

                (*Pause.*)

MICHAEL   You're right. Yes. We have no other choice. We
                just get on with it.

                (*He stands up, almost heroically.*)

                Top of Act One, Clive. Let's do this!

                (*He claps his hands.*)

EDDIE   Sorry to butt in . . . but we're two down I'm
                afraid.

MICHAEL   What? Who?

EDDIE   Hugo is getting changed and . . . no one knows
                where Sophie is.

MICHAEL   Oh, for God's sake. Has anyone tried ringing
               her?

               (*They look around. No one has.*)

               Fine!

               (*He takes out his mobile and dials a number.*)

               Straight to voicemail. Okay! Whilst we wait
               we'll do sound cues. Clive! Sound cues for Act
               One please!

ALISON   Oh, Michael . . . before I forget. This was in
               your pigeonhole. You must have missed it.

               (*He takes it from her and inspects it before
               crumpling it up and shoving it in his pocket.*)

MICHAEL   No, I didn't miss it. I just ignored it.

ALISON   Nothing wrong I hope?

MICHAEL   No, no. Nothing to worry about. Right! Clive,
               bring the lights down for the start of Act One,
               please.

               (MICHAEL *rushes off stage and comes back on
               with a script. He makes his way down the steps
               into the auditorium and takes his seat (reserved
               all evening in a suitable spot.*)

               You lot can stay on stage if you wish. Tell me
               what the cues sound like . . . volume etc. You
               know the score. Right, Clive. Lights! If I've
               asked you once I've asked you a hundred –

               (*All the lights snap out. Pitch black.*)

MICHAEL   What the bloody hell . . . ? I can't see a thing!

DIANA   For God's sake . . . I'm reading here! Hello?

MICHAEL   Clive?

                   (*Nothing.*)

                   CLIVE!!

                   (*Silence. A slight breeze can be heard through
                   the theatre.*)

ALISON   Is it me or is it suddenly very cold?

MICHAEL   Shhh! What's that . . . ?

                   (*We hear creaking floorboards, footsteps.
                   Somewhere in the upper depths of the theatre.
                   We then hear . . . as if carried on the breeze . . .*)

VOICE   Invite me in.

                   (*A slight tapping, somewhere in the top of the
                   theatre – like a tipped walking stick or cane on
                   the floor. Rhythmic. But quiet.*

                   Silence, before . . .

                   *The quick snap of the rope, as of someone has
                   hanged themselves and the rope tightens round
                   their throat. Choking.*

                   ALISON *screams.*)

EDDIE   What the bloody hell is going on?!

                   (*The window slams shut. The lights snap back
                   on. Silence. Everyone is in shock.*)

MICHAEL   Clive! What the hell was that?

(*Suddenly the doors from the foyer are flung open and* SOPHIE *comes dashing in. She is exceptionally elegantly dressed in her costume.*)

SOPHIE   Oh, thank God! You're here! I am so sorry. I know I'm late. So late. Michael, please forgive me. I lost track of time. I know you'll want to fire me but –

(*Beat.*)

Is everyone okay? Diana . . . are you all right? You look like death itself.

DIANA   I love this girl, I really do.

MICHAEL   We're fine, we just had a funny . . . we're fine. And don't worry, you're not going to get fired.

DIANA   Shouldn't we put that to a vote?

SOPHIE   I am so, so sorry, Michael. But hey! Here I am, ready to do with as you please.

(EDDIE *snorts.*)

MICHAEL   Yes . . . quite literally ready. Sophie, sweetheart. You didn't go into town in your costume did you?

SOPHIE   Erm . . . if I did . . . ? Is that a problem?

MICHAEL   (*Escorting her up onto the stage in a gentlemanly fashion.*) Well, yes. I'm afraid it is. I don't know how things are done in the States, but over here, actors never, ever go out anywhere in their costume. It's a sort of tradition. It ruins the illusion . . . fourth wall . . . see what I mean?

SOPHIE   Oh, no. I really am screwing up this evening aren't I?

DIANA	And we haven't even started rehearsing yet.
SOPHIE	What's that?
MICHAEL	No, no . . . don't worry. Just try not to go out like that again.
EDDIE	Where did you go for dinner?
SOPHIE	I went to a lovely little . . . what do you call them here . . . pub? Down the road. Dog and something? [*Or insert name of local, insalubrious hostelry.*] I had a craving for red meat so I had the steak. Delicious.
	(DIANA *throws her newspaper down in disgust.*)
EDDIE	You went to the [*Dog and Gun*], dressed like that?
SOPHIE	I sure did. I got some looks, I can tell you.
MICHAEL	No doubt.
SOPHIE	I am sorry, I just feel so fabulous in it I just hate taking it off.
MICHAEL	Well, I'm glad you feel so fabulous. And so you should. But quite apart from not letting the public see your costume, this dress cost almost half of our entire wardrobe budget so no more going to eat steak in pubs dressed like that, okay?
SOPHIE	Okay.
MICHAEL	Okay.
	(*Enter* HUGO. *Now dressed in his dinner jacket.*)
HUGO	Is everything okay? I thought I heard screaming. Oh . . . you've made it.

(*He gives* SOPHIE *a kiss on both cheeks.*)

Looking ravishing as ever. Hang on . . . I didn't
see you downstairs. How did you get changed
so quickly?

ALISON   She went out like that.

EDDIE   To the [*Dog and Gun*].

HUGO   Really? And lived to tell the tale?

DIANA   And to add insult to injury, she had a bloody
              steak!

              (HUGO *finds this very funny.*)

MICHAEL   Right! We're all finally here. So gather . . .
              gather, please.

              (*The cast finish any small talk they feel they
              need to enter into . . .*)

              Thank you!

              (*They come to order and* MICHAEL *addresses
              them.*)

              Okay. So hear we are. Eve of opening
              night. And I hope you feel as terrified and
              underprepared as I do.

HUGO   Crikey. Hardly the Gettysburg address, is it?

MICHAEL   But that's okay – a little fear is allowed. In fact
              I would be alarmed if we were feeling anything
              other than completely terrified. When I directed
              three consecutive shows in the West End . . .

EDDIE   Here we go . . .

MICHAEL   I felt completely terrified for each one. Under-rehearsed, under-prepared and under pressure. I didn't sleep for weeks.

                   (*We get the impression they have all heard this before . . .*)

                   But you know what happened? We got on with it. We had no choice. In my very core I know we are on the cusp of something very, very special, yes? The revival of a lost classic and with your talents we will make it a hit. A damn big hit! Yes?

                   (*Mumblings of agreement.*)

                   And, I know tomorrow night is just a preview and you are all experienced enough to know in the back of your minds that if we really aren't ready we can delay opening. That's what previews are for. But I want you to get those thoughts out of your mind immediately! We are ready. The revival of *Scared to Death* by Lucian O'Keefe is long overdue and we hold it here in our hands. We are the lucky custodians of something exceptional. And it's okay to be nervous, this play deals with death, murder and the supernatural . . . a little bit of fear is not only expected, it's necessary . . . adds . . . atmosphere.

                   (*The lights flicker. Distant tapping.*)

EDDIE   What the hell is that?

MICHAEL   Very funny, Clive? Thank you!

DIANA   I can't help feeling, Michael my dear, that the fear of the undead is quite different from the fear of not knowing what the hell we're meant to be doing and not knowing our lines.

MICHAEL   You all know what you're doing, I can see that.

DIANA   (*Pointedly.*) Some of us do.

MICHAEL   Now listen. I have complete faith in all of you.
              We have tonight to run through the show,
              ironing out any little problems and we have all
              of tomorrow as well. More than enough time. I
              can't remember if I have ever told you but when
              I directed *Hay Fever* in the West End we didn't
              even have time to do a full dress rehearsal!
              Can you imagine . . . but that show ran for two
              years! Two years! Diana, you were there . . .
              remember the uncertainty, the abject fear we all
              felt on that first night?

DIANA   Difference being, my darling that we had Noel
              Coward's words to fall back on. A proven
              classic. Hay Fever was never lost, it was too
              good to lose.

MICHAEL   I refuse to start questioning the quality of the
              play! Have faith in it as I have faith in you.
              You're marvellous, the play's marvellous . . . it's
              all going to be marvellous. We'll spend a few
              weeks here and then we'll move into the West
              End. Visualise it and it will happen.

              (MICHAEL *looks at his watch.*)

              Now, you're all ready. You've all had your
              union-regulated break and we're going back to
              work. I want to go from Diana's entrance and
              then into the séance scene.

              (*Clapping his hands . . .*)

              Come on!

HUGO   We're not going from the top?

MICHAEL   No, we're not going from the top. Otherwise
               I would have said, we're going from the top. I
               didn't. We're going from Diana's entrance.

               (*They all start chatting together as they get
               ready.* ALISON *exits SL and a moment later comes
               back on struggling with a circular table . . .*)

ALISON   This is on, I assume. Hugo and Eddie have set
               this up by the time Diana enters.

MICHAEL   Yes, yes of course, very good.

               (*He goes to help her.*)

MICHAEL   Eddie, Hugo! Bring the chairs and the cloth will
               you? Diana?!

DIANA   (*Now off.*) What?

MICHAEL   Ready for your entrance?

DIANA   Thank you, yes. I have done this before you
               know.

SOPHIE   So I am . . . erm . . . ?

MICHAEL   On stage. Remember? You are on stage. This is
               Diana's entrance. Zelma van Tanzen arrives at
               the house. Okay?

SOPHIE   Okay. Should I let her in?

MICHAEL   No, no. We haven't started yet. Just wait. You
               are sitting in a chair. This chair. (*He escorts her.*)
               We'll the run the scene a few lines before she
               arrives.

SOPHIE   Right. Great. Here I am.

               (*She sits down.* EDDIE *and* HUGO *bring on a
               scarlet tablecloth and five chairs. The circular*

table is set centre stage. The chairs are placed
around the table, the tablecloth over the table.
ALISON, MICHAEL, HUGO *and* EDDIE *do all this.*)

MICHAEL   Lovely. Excellent, looks perfect, don't you
                 think? Right! Places, everyone.

                 (MICHAEL *picks up his script and descends into*
                 the auditorium and takes his seat.)

                 Is this the right lighting state? Clive?

                 (*The lights change.*)

                 Good. Thank you. Okay . . . we'll go from . . .
                 Betsy "I just can't imagine . . . " Okay? When
                 you're ready.

                 (HUGO *picks up two glasses and hands one to*
                 EDDIE.)

EDDIE   Oh, yeah. Thanks.

                 (HUGO *takes his place by the mantelpiece.* EDDIE
                 raises the window and then sits on the window
                 seat. ALISON *sits in the opposite chair to* SOPHIE.)

MICHAEL   Thank you. Now . . . when you're ready,
                 Sophie.

SOPHIE   Mmm?

MICHAEL   "I just can't imagine . . . "

SOPHIE   Oh, yes! Right.

                 (*She 'steadies' herself.*)

                 (*Practising her English accent to get into it*) The
                 rain in Spain stays mainly in the plain. Hello,
                 your Majesty. England. I live in England, Albert.

EDDIE	Is she quite all right?
MICHAEL	Sophie, darling? What the hell are you doing?
SOPHIE	Accent work . . . it seems to help.
MICHAEL	I'm sure, but maybe just in your head from now on, is that all right?
SOPHIE	Oh, sure.

(*She closes her eyes and nods as she does her bizarre ritual. They all wait. She opens her eyes and smiles.*)

MICHAEL	Ready?
SOPHIE	Ready . . . I mean (*In an English accent.*) Ready, thank you.
MICHAEL	Excellent. (*Long pause.*) Sophie!
SOPHIE	Oh shit! Yeah . . . erm . . .

(SOPHIE's *English accent is passable at best. She is attempting, of course, to achieve an RP accent, which her colleagues deliver admirably. Her major issues lie with vowel sounds and confusion thereof. For example, one of her major habits is to pronounce what should be a flat 'e' sound – as in romantic – with a rounded 'ah' sound – as in arse! Rom-are-ntic. The trick is to highlight this when necessary and not make it distract from the actual dialogue.*)

BETSY	I just can't imagine what she's going to look like.
GERALD	Just like one of us, I suppose. Wouldn't you say, Timothy?
TIMOTHY	She was perfectly normal looking when I met her.

PENELOPE   I do hope not. That would be most disappointing.

GERALD   Ha! You really are a card. You want her to be
                some sort of Eastern mystic don't you? You're a
                terrible romantic.

BETSY   I don't see anything even remotely romantic
                about this. In fact I am not entirely sure this is
                not pure folly. (*She pronounces this like 'foley'.*)

MICHAEL   FOLLY. FO – LLY.

SOPHIE   Right, thank you. Shit.

BETSY   In fact I am not entirely sure this is not pure folly.

                (*She smiles as she gets this right.*)

TIMOTHY   Folly? Hardly. At the very least it's an adventure.

PENELOPE   An adventure? Betsy, dear. Did you know you
                were marrying such a man?

BETSY   In what way, Penelope?

PENELOPE   Well, dear little Timothy. My darling little
                brother, the country solicitor and respected
                professional is in fact a meddler in the dark
                arts? Who would have thought!

TIMOTHY   To be perfectly honest, sister dearest, I don't for
                one moment believe there are any dark arts to
                be meddled in.

GERALD   Really? Then what are we all doing here?

TIMOTHY   Well, it's all a bit of fun, don't you think? A
                chance to get together and get a little tight.
                Have some fun. What?

GERALD   Fun? One hopes. But tell me, wasn't this, van
                Tanzen lady the one who in fact approached
                you?

BETSY   She was. Tell them, Timothy.

TIMOTHY   Well, yes. If you must know. It was, what, a
                fortnight or so ago and I was in the village, I
                can't remember what doing.

BETSY   You were posting a parcel to your mother. The
                lampshade we had found in Gregson's.

TIMOTHY   Oh, that's right. The lampshade. Yes, I was
                leaving the Post Office and was just about to
                get into my motor when this lady appeared
                beside me. Almost out of nowhere.

GERALD   Oh, come now, Old Boy. There's really no need
                to hyperbolise. Out of nowhere, my hat!

TIMOTHY   I'm telling you, it was as if she had appeared.
                Simply appeared. On my honour I hadn't seen
                her in the street but here she was, next to me,
                closer than you are to me now.

PENELOPE   And then what happened?

TIMOTHY   Well, the damndest thing. She asked me,
                without any introduction or generally accepted
                pleasantries, and in that funny accent of hers
                – you'll notice when she arrives – if I were the
                man who had just moved into Cricklethorpe
                Manor. Well, of course I was very pleased to
                say that I was, that my wife and I had moved in
                only a week or so before.

BETSY   And tell them what happened when you
                mentioned me.

TIMOTHY   Yes, I was coming to that. As soon as I
                mentioned I had a wife, her face turned to

stone. "Your wife?" she asked, "Is she quite all right?" Well, I didn't know what on earth she meant but I put her mind at rest and said that she was perfectly all right when I left her this morning. Except that she had turned rather furious on discovering I had marched my dirty wellington boots into the hallway after walking the dogs this morning.

(*They all laugh.*)

BETSY   Mrs Bray had only just swept and cleaned! It's a habit I hope to release him from, eventually. You terrible man.

(TIMOTHY *kisses his wife on the forehead and stands behind her with his arm on her shoulder. Tender.*)

GERALD   Carry on. What did this van Tanzen lady say after that?

TIMOTHY   Well, she went on to tell me that I had bought a house with a dark past. That the original owner had built the place for his wife, as a gift. But as soon as they moved in, she had fallen ill and died.

PENELOPE   Oh, how dreadfully sad.

TIMOTHY   But there's more. She said that he had been turned mad with grief and had killed himself. Strychnine I think she said.

GERALD   Good God!

TIMOTHY   And that ever since, everyone who had lived here had only lasted a few months before having to leave.

PENELOPE   Why?

TIMOTHY   Because he is said to haunt the place.

GERALD   Poppycock!

TIMOTHY   Well, of course it is. But she did know the
               strangest thing. She asked whether I'd got a
               good price on the place. As we all know, I did.
               She said that was because the previous owners
               couldn't sell and get out fast enough.

GERALD   Because of this old boy's ghost?

TIMOTHY   Precisely. She went on to tell me that the ghost
               of this chap is still wrought with grief and if a
               happily married couple move in his jealously
               turns to rage and he sets his sights on turning
               the wife mad with fear until she dies.

PENELOPE   He literally wants her to be . . .

TIMOTHY   Scared to death.

               (*Silence.* BETSY *shivers.*)

BETSY   Oh, I really don't like it.

TIMOTHY   Oh, come now, my love. It's all tosh. But a bit
               of fun nonetheless.

GERALD   So why is she coming here tonight?

TIMOTHY   Because she offered her services to me. She
               said she had offered the same to the previous
               owners but they had turned her down.

PENELOPE   What sort of services?

TIMOTHY   A séance.

PENELOPE   Ah, hence the table and chairs.

TIMOTHY   Exactly.

GERALD	Good, I thought it was a pretty poor show for a dinner table!
TIMOTHY	She told me that she has . . . certain powers. That she can contact the restless spirit of this man and put him to rest forever. And that this would save my wife's sanity, maybe indeed her life.
PENELOPE	Good gracious.
TIMOTHY	I don't believe it for a moment. Any of it. But these séances, they're all the rage in London and as I knew you two were coming to raise a toast to our first marital home, I thought, why not combine the two and make an evening of it? What fun!
BETSY	As long as it is just that. Fun.
TIMOTHY	Betsy is not too sure about it, I'm afraid.
GERALD	Well, you can't really blame her, it's her life at stake.
PENELOPE	Gerald, that's not funny.
GERALD	And, not a bad deal for this van Tanzen either, I suppose.
BETSY	How do you mean?
GERALD	Well, she comes here. Does her party piece, gets a sherry and I assume turns a nice profit at the same time.
TIMOTHY	Well, that's the thing. A sherry perhaps, but she refuses to take any money for her services. She said her payment will be the simple fact of knowing she had saved the life of a young woman.

GERALD	Really? My word. Makes you think I suppose, doesn't it?
TIMOTHY	What does?
GERALD	I mean to say, what do we really know about these things? When all is said and done, there are plenty of occurrences in this world that defy rational explanation.
TIMOTHY	You mean you really believe there could be something in this? Come off it, Old Boy!
GERALD	Hardly. But . . .
PENELOPE	Are you quite all right, dear?
GERALD	Just for a moment imagine that it's true. That this chap, this evil spirit . . . is in the room with us now. Amongst us. Watching us.
	(*Silence.*
	Suddenly a loud knocking at the door. They all jump and the ladies scream.)
TIMOTHY	Good God! Damn near had a heart attack.
	(ZELMA VAN TANZEN *appears at the window, she pokes her head inside.*)
ZELMA	I am here, ladies and gentlemen.
TIMOTHY	We heard, Mrs van Tanzen.
ZELMA	Miss van Tanzen. Never married. Never wanted to.
TIMOTHY	Right. I see. Well, lovely to have you here. Come on, I'll let you in the front door.

ZELMA	Well, I wasn't expecting to come through this window.
TIMOTHY	Ha! No, don't worry.

(TIMOTHY *goes to the front door. Before he opens it he addresses the others . . .*)

Well, here we go.

(*He opens the door.* ZELMA VAN TANZEN *breezes in. Elaborately dressed, holding an equally elaborate bag on her arm.*)

ZELMA	Good eve–

(*She stops dead, and breathes in deeply.*)

ZELMA	Yes. Yes. He's here. Oh, yes, he is here and he is strong. Stronger even than I had feared.
GERALD	(*Introducing himself.*) Gerald Makepeace and this is my wife . . .
ZELMA	No, no. We don't have time for such things. (*She sees* BETSY.) Ah! You are she.
BETSY	I'm sorry?
TIMOTHY	Yes, this is my wife, Betsy.

(ZELMA *approaches her and softly strokes her face.*)

ZELMA	Yes, my dear. He is very fond of you. Very fond. Be brave. Be strong. And I will save you.
BETSY	Thank you, I am sure.
TIMOTHY	Yes, we're all grateful for that. Sherry?
ZELMA	No! I never touch a drop when I am channelling. Tonight of all nights, I have to

be clear in mind and body. I fear this will be tougher than I had imagined. (*Back to* BETSY.) Such beauty, such unadulterated beauty. You are, quite simply, perfect.

BETSY   Gosh. That's very kind. You're making me blush. I'm as red as a tomato. (*She pronounces this in the American style.*)

MICHAEL   Tom – ah – to! Tom – ah – to!

SOPHIE   Oh, damn! I am so sorry. (*Repeating it.*) Tom – ah – to. Tom – ah – to. It just feels so unnatural for me.

DIANA   Is that simply vowel sounds or the art of acting more generally?

MICHAEL   Thank you, Diana!

ALISON   You were doing so well.

MICHAEL   Come on, come on. Let's carry on, please. Just imagine it's first night and I am your audience.

DIANA   Pretty accurate representation by all accounts.

HUGO   We're not selling?

DIANA   No. Thank God.

MICHAEL   Carry on! Red as a tomato!

BETSY   Gosh, that's very kind. You're making me blush. I'm as red as a tom-ah-to.

ZELMA   Hush, my child. You are safe now, trust me to do my work and I will save your very soul.

GERALD   I say, this is all a little bleak isn't it?

TIMOTHY   Just let her have her fun, old boy.

ZELMA   Fun? Fun? If you have invited me here to have
                 fun, you have underestimated the power of
                 the dark arts and their capabilities. You have
                 purchased and decided to live within a cursed
                 home where your wife's very life is at stake.
                 Trust me, in no way is this fun nor is it for your
                 entertainment. If you wish me to do my job,
                 you must allow me to channel the spirit of an
                 evil, vindictive man. A man who wishes harm
                 and pain in order to relieve his own. Do not
                 treat this evening's events with anything except
                 the gravest respect. Do you understand?

PENELOPE   I should say so.

TIMOTHY   Well, yes. Of course. I'm terribly sorry, I'm sure.
                 Gerald?

GERALD   Mm?

TIMOTHY   Are you ready to treat this evening with the
                 gravest respect?

GERALD   God, yes! Most certainly, old chap. It's your
                 wife's life at stake after all.

ZELMA   Good. Then we shall proceed. May I ask you all
                 to gather around the table?

                 (Slightly uneasily and seeing which of them will
                 have the courage to do it first, they take their
                 places around the table.)

TIMOTHY   I hope this table is to your satisfaction, Miss
                 Van Tanzen?

ZELMA   It will serve.

TIMOTHY   Excellent.

PENELOPE	It won't get damaged will it? It was father's, he brought it back from India. I would be heartbroken to see any harm come to it.
ZELMA	As long as we keep the circle strong and our minds free, no harm will come to any of us or any object in the room.
TIMOTHY	Excellent, sounds good to me.
BETSY	Gosh, I do hope you're right. What with this being done on my behalf.
ZELMA	Lights! We are too bright in here. Mr Grey, please.

(TIMOTHY *rises . . .*)

TIMOTHY	How dark would you like it, Mrs Van Tanzen?
ZELMA	Leave only a glow.
TIMOTHY	Right ho.

(*He dims the lights from the wall.*)

How's that?

ZELMA	Excellent.

(*She reaches into her bag and withdraws a small, hanging bell, placing it in the centre of the table as* TIMOTHY *retakes his seat.*)

PENELOPE	What is that, may I ask?
ZELMA	This, ladies and gentleman is a spirit bell.
GERALD	Dainty little thing isn't it?
ZELMA	This . . . dainty little thing . . . is over three hundred years old and has been handed down through the female line of my family, all of

whom have had 'the gift'. This bell is from the Orient, made by the master Spirit Talker, Xuan Liu, who it is said, cleared over a thousand spirits in her time. Gifted to a distant relative of mine in eighteenth century Prussia, this bell has alerted many séances to their arrival.

BETSY   Whose arrival?

ZELMA   The spirits. At the ringing of this bell, we know we are not alone.

(*They all stare at the bell for a moment.*)

And now, we will join hands. Create a circle, come on!

(*They do so, joining hands around the table.*)

A strong circle that he can't infiltrate. At no point can we break contact. No matter what I do, or say or even if I appear to be in pain, keep the circle intact. Do you all understand?

(*They all nod, sombrely.*)

Good. Now we shall begin.

(ZELMA *takes a deep breath, closes her eyes and looks up the ceiling.*)

Oh, spirits of the netherplace, the near distance and the black, I call upon thee, I ask thee to come amongst us and . . .

(*The bell rings.* DIANA *stops and looks confused as do all the others, looking at the bell.*)

MICHAEL   Not now, Clive!

HUGO   No. That was the actual bell.

MICHAEL	Don't be ridiculous.
EDDIE	No, I really think it was.
MICHAEL	Well, one of you must have knocked the table. Clive! Make a note to have a look at that bell. Take the ringer, or whatever it's called out . . . sound effects only. Yes? Right, carry on.
ZELMA	I ask thee to come amongst us and alert us to thy presence, allow us to know you, feel you and speak with you. Oh, spirits, I am your channel, your vessel and your . . .

(The bell rings again.)

MICHAEL	Whoever the joker is, just bloody stop it!
ALISON	I don't think any of us are touching it, Michael.
MICHAEL	Then it's a gust of wind or a draft or any other cliché I can think of . . . either way can we just proceed, please?
ZELMA	Oh spirits, I am your channel, your vessel and your guide into our world. I ask you to join us, speak with us and be at one with us.

(The bell rings vigorously.)

HUGO	What the hell is going on?

(He picks up the ringing bell . . .)

HUGO	This is weird . . . you have to admit.

(The bell suddenly flies across the room. [Alternatively, a picture falls from the wall or similar. It has to be violent in its speed and effect, shocking]. All goes quiet.

Silence

The tapping can be heard again, distant.)

ALISON   What the hell is that?

             *(It gets closer and closer and louder and louder
             . . . it stops.*

             Blackout. Appropriate ad lib . . .)

MICHAEL   Clive?! Clive?! What the hell is going on? Clive?

SOPHIE   I'm sorry, but I really don't like this.

HUGO   Shhh!

             (The bell rings again.

             *Suddenly, the door flies open at the back of the
             auditorium.*

             Enter GILES

             The lights come back up with a snap.)

GILES   *(Marching through the aisle.)* Stop! For God's
             sake, stop!

MICHAEL   Who the hell are you?

GILES   You haven't done it yet, have you?

ALISON   Done what?

GILES   The séance? Have you completed the séance
             scene?

DIANA   I was giving it a good go.

GILES   But you didn't finish it? You didn't get to the
             end of Zelma's speech?

HUGO   Who the hell is this guy?

GILES   Did you?

MICHAEL   No, we didn't!

GILES   Thank God.

MICHAEL   May I alert you to the fact that you have
               interrupted a dress rehearsal for a production
               that opens here tomorrow night.

GILES   And by doing so, I have saved your lives,
               indeed your very souls.

MICHAEL   Excuse me, but who the bloody hell are you?

GILES   Giles Heath.

MICHAEL   Oh, I should have guessed!

EDDIE   Who on earth is Giles Heath?

HUGO   How the hell should I know?

GILES   I trust you have received my letters?

MICHAEL   I have, all fourteen . . .

               (*He remembers the letter in his pocket and
               takes it out and throws it at* GILES.)

MICHAEL   FIFTEEN! Fifteen of your damn letters.

GILES   And yet here you are. Ignoring my warnings?

MICHAEL   Nonsense, utter nonsense! You really think I am
               going to pull a production of a play because of
               the wild ramblings of a lunatic with too much
               time on his hands and a ludicrous imagination?
               And now you have the audacity to march in
               and interrupt rehearsals at a critical stage. You
               astound me!

GILES   Critical is the word.

Michael	You're mad.
Diana	What on earth is going on?
Giles	I am Professor Giles Heath of the University of Bristol, theatre historian.
Hugo	Theatre historian, eh? Crikey, he may even have heard of you, Diana.
Diana	Piss off, you cocky little shit.
Michael	This man is a lunatic, intent on preventing this show from going ahead on the basis of unproven nonsense and hearsay.
Giles	Unproven? Hardly, I have given you the facts and if you've read my letters you will know them.
Michael	I gave up at letter number three.
Giles	Then you're a fool and you're placing the life of your actors and, may I add, your audience in peril.
Michael	I want you to leave, immediately.
Giles	And I want you to call a halt to this production immediately.
Michael	That's not going to happen.
Giles	Don't be an idiot! What I have told you is true. All of it and yet you choose to ignore me.
Michael	I most certainly do, now leave!
Alison	Michael, what's he talking about?
Giles	You haven't told them?
Michael	Of course I haven't. There's nothing to tell.

GILES   This play is cursed, as is this very theatre.
               By putting the two together again you are
               awakening forces of such evil and despair
               you can't begin to even comprehend the
               consequences.

MICHAEL   What rubbish! It's a play, that's all. A piece of
               entertainment.

GILES   A play that possesses a scene written
               specifically to raise the spirits of the dead. In
               here, in this very theatre.

MICHAEL   (*Trying to manhandle him.*) Get out! Get off my
               stage and leave!

GILES   You're making a terrible mistake. If you perform
               this play, even rehearse it in this theatre, you
               will be endangering all those who perform in it
               as well as those who are watching. It's a crime.

MICHAEL   You're the only criminal in here, spouting
               nonsense and risking the success of a production.
               I could have you arrested. Now get out!

               (*He pushes him down the steps into the
               auditorium.* GILES *swings around, catches sight
               of the spirit bell on the floor.*)

GILES   A spirit bell. Did you rehearse with a spirit bell?

DIANA   What if we did?

GILES   In here? And did it ring?

               (*Pause, no one wants to answer.*)

               Did it ring?!

EDDIE   Yes, but that could have been anything . . .

GILES   Then it's started. Dear God, you have to listen
                    to me. Please, you can't continue with this play.
                    He's waiting, he's always here, waiting to be
                    asked in. And this play does exactly that . . .
                    asks him in. And once that has happened . . .
                    evil descends.

MICHAEL   Get out.

HUGO   Hang on, Michael. I think I speak for everyone
                    when I say we want to hear him out. We have a
                    right to know what's going on. We are, after all,
                    in this play.

MICHAEL   See what you've done? (*To the cast.*) It's
                    rubbish, all of it. Listening to what he's got to
                    say is a waste of time and time is a precious
                    commodity for us.

SOPHIE   Still, I think we deserve to know what's going on.

MICHAEL   But . . . oh, for God's sake!

GILES   They're right. Let me tell them and then they
                    can make up their minds as to whether they
                    wish to proceed with this production.

MICHAEL   Fine! Go ahead. But may I say, you are all
                    intelligent and well-informed members of
                    society. Bear this in mind as you listen to this
                    madman.

                    (GILES *makes his way back onto the stage and
                    slowly picks up the spirit bell, inspects it, places
                    is back on the table and begins . . .*)

GILES   Alderwick Haye. None of you will have heard
                    of him. A name lost to the dark recesses of
                    theatre history but a name you have to be
                    accustomed to this evening. Alderwick Haye
                    was the original actor manager of this theatre
                    from 1875 until his death five years later. An

egotistical tyrant of a man, he ran this theatre with a rod of iron and was famous throughout the town. Always in his large black cape, and always walking with his steel-tipped cane – everywhere he went people could hear him coming. Tap, tap, tap.

In 1879 he married a young actress within his company, Rose Blarney, a beautiful, star-struck girl thirty years his junior. The marriage was fated. She married for status and security and more than likely because she was too scared to turn him down. He married for obsession. They say he followed her home every night, tap, tap, tapping his cane behind her so she knew he was there. He didn't love her, he craved her. He wanted to own her.

Late one night, Haye was at home alone, Rose was away, he believed, visiting her mother. He realised he'd left his cane in his dressing room. He made the short walk back to the theatre from his home and having retrieved his cane he was about to leave when he heard something below, on the stage. He heard Rose's voice. Then Laughter. And a man's voice. The voice of the young stagehand. Making sure not to be heard, Haye made his way to the back of the auditorium and stood in the darkness as he watched his wife undress and make love to this man. Mad with rage, Haye dashed onto the stage and with the handle of his cane struck the young man across the head, killing him. He then went for Rose. Unable to deal with what he had done, Alderwick Haye took himself into the rafters above the stage, and hanged himself. But Rose was not dead. She was found the next day, delirious with grief, her lover's body beside her, her husband's body hanging lifeless above her.

ALISON   That's horrible.

GILES   But there's more. As Haye threw himself to his
            death, Rose opened her eyes. As he writhed
            and struggled, life ebbing from his body she
            just watched and did nothing as he slowly,
            dreadfully died. And now his spirit, his angry,
            bitter and twisted spirit remains . . . here in this
            theatre, waiting for Rose's return. So he can
            drag her to hell with him.

            (*Pause.*)

HUGO   Well, I'm no professor of theatre history but
            even I can tell you he'll be waiting a bloody
            long time.

SOPHIE   And this is why we shouldn't do this play . . .
            because this theatre is haunted?

GILES   Not only is this theatre haunted, but the play
            itself is haunted.

DIANA   What the hell do you mean by that?

MICHAEL   Oh, this is where it gets really good.

GILES   Your director may jest but what I am telling you
            is the truth.

ALISON   But how can a play, a work of fiction, be
            haunted?

GILES   Ah, but is it a work of fiction? That's what
            you've got to ask. Lucian O'Keefe was a
            struggling and penniless playwright in 1946.
            But O'Keefe was also a keen student of theatre
            history so it was only a matter of time before
            he stumbled upon the story of this theatre
            and of the tragic tale of Alderwick Haye and
            Rose Blarney. So struck was he by this story
            that he visited this theatre a number of times

and having a keen interest in the Occult,
O'Keefe was desperate to prove the stories
true. Rumours were that he had an encounter
with the spirit of Haye one evening on this very
stage and this is when the idea hit him. What
better way to guarantee success than write a
ghost play . . . with a real ghost? This is how
Scared to Death was born. Think about the plot
. . . a young couple move into a supposedly
haunted house and with the help of a medium
. . . Zelma Van Tanzen, they summon up the
spirit of a deranged, evil and grief stricken man
intent on taking a soul with him to hell. It's the
story of Alderwick Haye in a different guise. So
O'Keefe studied the dark arts and was able to
write a perfectly accurate séance scene into the
play. The scene you perform in this play is not a
work of fiction, it is in fact a real séance . . . the
exact way to bring Alderwick Haye's physical
form back to this theatre.

DIANA   But we've rehearsed that scene countless times,
               how come he hasn't appeared yet?

GILES   Because you haven't rehearsed it here, have you?

HUGO   Well, we were trying but . . .

GILES   But you were interrupted. The bell rang, I
               assume? That's him. That's Alderwick Haye,
               growing in strength as you prepare to welcome
               him home.

EDDIE   But surely then, when they performed it the first
               time, in 1946 . . . what happened?

GILES   O'Keefe directed the play himself and made
               sure the séance scene wasn't written correctly
               until opening night. So when it was performed
               Haye returned. The play of course, seemed to
               go well except for a few strange occurrences.
               The actors would sense someone they didn't

know off stage. Audience members began
to leave as they became aware of a strange
presence in the auditorium. Lights and sound
effects went wrong. And then . . . Alderwick
Haye was seen, on stage. His grotesque and
twisted face, just as it was when he died, filled
with fury and hatred.

HUGO   Seen? Where?

GILES   At that window there. Staring in . . . looking for
              a soul to take to hell.

              (*They all stare at the window. It slams shut.*)

MICHAEL   Clive! That window is now a priority!

GILES   Of course, the play was stopped. The cast
              refused to go on for the second half and most of
              the audience had left. But no one could find the
              playwright and the director. Lucian O'Keefe had
              vanished.

ALISON   He'd run away?

GILES   He had tried. His body was later found in the
              farthest corner of the basement, where the
              dressing rooms are now. His face frozen in fear.
              His eyes wide open. His mouth stretched in a
              voiceless scream. He had, quite literally, been
              scared to death.

              (*Silence.*)

GILES   The play was lost. Never to be performed
              again. Until you . . . you fool, decided to try
              and rekindle your dwindling career by reviving
              it. You're doing exactly what O'Keefe did and
              it will end in the same way. Mark my words, if
              you perform this play, more specifically, if you
              perform the séance scene as is written . . . one
              of you will die.

(MICHAEL *claps sarcastically.*)

MICHAEL   Bravo! Bravo! If I get a performance that good
               out of any of you lot, I will be delighted. Such
               commitment, such honesty.

GILES   You can't let this go ahead!

MICHAEL   You're ridiculous. Lucian O'Keefe was just
               unlucky. His play is a lost classic, a thriller
               of the highest order and, more importantly,
               commercially hot. And if you, any of you,
               think that I am going to pull the plug on this
               production on the basis of a schoolboy ghost
               story, you're very much mistaken.

ALISON   Shouldn't we treat it with a little care, Michael?
               These things . . . we don't know what we're
               dealing with.

HUGO   Oh come off it! We're dealing with a play.
               Simple as that. Mr Heath. Sorry, Professor
               Heath. Thank you for this but we're opening a
               play tomorrow night and we're severely behind
               schedule. We've just got to get on with it.

MICHAEL   Exactly, that's the spirit. (*Realising the poor
               joke.*) Boom, boom!

HUGO   What's the alternative? We just pack up and go
               home? I for one have nothing to go home for.
               I have a six-month contract for this play and I
               intend to see it through. Diana?

DIANA   (*Perhaps more bravely than she truly feels.*)
               Quite right. Nonsense.

GILES   You're all mad! You simply can't let this happen.

MICHAEL   We can and we shall. Stay and watch if you
               like, see that nothing happens and perhaps
               then you will leave me and my play alone.

Right! Everyone, get ready for the séance scene, please.

(*The cast begin to get ready and assemble themselves for the séance scene.*)

GILES   Stop! No . . . you don't know what you're dealing with.

MICHAEL   I am dealing with a play that is behind schedule and a mad man intent on scuppering it. Now stay and watch, or get out.

GILES   (*Making his way back through the auditorium.*) Fools! You're all fools. This can only end in tragedy and death.

MICHAEL   Thank you, Professor. Get back to your history and let me make mine.

GILES   (*Turning before he leaves, in the doorway.*) May God protect you. May he protect you all.

(*He exits.*)

MICHAEL   Now there is a true drama queen. Are we ready?

(*The cast all let him know, via ad lib, that they are ready.*

MICHAEL *takes his seat in the auditorium.*)

Excellent. From the start of the séance please. When you're ready, Diana. Thank you.

(*Pause.*)

DIANA   Here goes nothing.

(*She takes a breath and . . .*)

ZELMA   Oh, spirits of the netherplace, the near distance
             and the black, I call upon thee, I ask thee to
             come amongst us and alert us to thy presence,
             allow us to know you, feel you and speak with
             you. Oh, spirits, I am your channel, your vessel
             and your guide. I ask you to join us, speak with
             us and be at one with us.

             (*Tapping, now louder than before.* DIANA
             hesitates.)

MICHAEL   Carry on!

ZELMA   You are welcome, allow yourself to join us . . .

VOICE   Invite me in.

MICHAEL   It's nothing! Carry on!

HUGO   Are you sure . . . I mean –

MICHAEL   Finish the scene or you're all fired!

ZELMA   Entrust me with your wandering soul and find
             yourself walking with us.

VOICE   Invite me in.

ZELMA   Enter! I invite you to enter and walk with us side
             by side!

             (*The lights flicker, the spirit bell rings and rings
             and rings, tapping grows louder and suddenly*
             DIANA *leaps up from the table, almost violently.
             The others scream and leap away from the
             table.* DIANA *is seemingly having some sort of fit;
             her eyes and mouth are stretched wide.*)

HUGO   Diana! Bloody hell, Michael . . . do something!

             (MICHAEL *stands, unable to move.* DIANA *falls to
             the floor and her fellow cast members rush to*

her aid. ALISON *takes a cushion from the settee and places it under her head.*)

ALISON   Darling, are you all right?

DIANA   I'm so sorry . . . I just don't know . . .

            (*The spirit bell rings.*

            The ghost of ALDERWICK HAYE *appears in the auditorium, unnoticed by the cast.*)

HUGO   This is ridiculous! Bloody ridiculous. Michael, you've got to call an end to this.

MICHAEL   (*In a daze.*) Mm?

HUGO   Michael! We can't go on now, surely?

MICHAEL   Of course we can. We must! This is all . . . just hokum. Diana . . . sweetheart, do you need a doctor before we carry on?

EDDIE   Of course she bloody does!

DIANA   (*Struggling to her feet.*) Don't be absurd, I haven't seen a doctor in my life. All I need is a strong coffee and a fag.

MICHAEL   Now there's a pro for you!

ALISON   Darling, surely you can't be thinking you can still rehearse?

DIANA   What else is there to do? I'm afraid my love I am of an age where things occasionally . . . spasm. No doubt it was a reaction to that dreadful vegetarian food I was forced to eat. Give me five minutes, Michael and I'll be back on track.

MICHAEL   You're a star. Right . . . everyone take five
               minutes and we'll carry on. Clive, I want to set
               up for the spirit cabinet scene. Clive! Clive!

               (*Suddenly* CLIVE *comes rushing in from the back
               of the auditorium. He enters with a shocking
               bang and carries two pots of paint.*)

CLIVE   Shit! Shit! Shit! I am so sorry . . . Michael, I just
               can't apologise enough. Please don't sack me . . .
               Shit! I am so sorry.

MICHAEL   Sorry about what, exactly?

CLIVE   Being so late. I went to pick up more paint for
               the doorframe. Ah, yes. The receipt . . .

               (*He unceremoniously hands a receipt to* MICHAEL
               that he finds in his pocket.)

               . . . but they couldn't find my sodding order,
               could they? And when they did eventually find
               it they'd given me the wrong sodding colour
               so off they went again for twenty minutes and
               then when I did get the . . . Blah blah blah
               . . . Anyway I'm late and I really am . . . so
               sorry. But I'm here now! Right! I'll finish the
               doorframe in the morning, I'll get up into the
               box and we'll get going, yeah? From the séance
               scene I guess, Michael?

               (*Pause. Everyone slowly looks up to the box.*)

CLIVE   Michael? Guys . . . is everything okay?

               (*Silence Lights snap to blackout.*

               End of Act One.)

ACT TWO

As the audience settle down and lights dim . . .

A huge crack of thunder and the sound of torrential rain. TIMOTHY *sits with a drink looking rather replete.* GERALD *stands by the window (now closed) and looks out. Jazz plays quietly from the gramophone.*

A moment of quietude.

A flash of lightning.

GERALD	One . . . two . . . three . . . four . . . five . . .
	(*A crack of thunder, more distant this time.*)
	It's moving on, I think.
TIMOTHY	Mm?
GERALD	The storm. I believe it's moving on.
TIMOTHY	Jolly good.
	(*Pause.* GERALD *moves and looks towards upstairs.*)
TIMOTHY	Drink?
GERALD	I think so. I'll help myself.
TIMOTHY	Please do.
	(GERALD *goes and pours himself a drink and stands by the fireplace.*)
TIMOTHY	Are you warm enough old chap?
GERALD	Oh, fine. Thank you.
TIMOTHY	Just let me know and I'll put another log on.

GERALD   Not on my account.

TIMOTHY   Wouldn't be any trouble. Just let me know.

GERALD   Right-ho.

            (*Pause.*)

            What do you think they're doing?

TIMOTHY   God knows.

GERALD   They've been up there for a while.

TIMOTHY   You know what women are.

GERALD   I suppose we do.

TIMOTHY   They'll find anything to make a drama out of
            and then find anything from that to make a
            conversation.

GERALD   Indeed.

TIMOTHY   Do you like this?

GERALD   What's that?

TIMOTHY   The music.

GERALD   Oh, I see yes. Is it the American chap?

TIMOTHY   Yes, that's the one. Top notch in my mind.

            (*Pause.*)

TIMOTHY   Something good did come from having all the
            yanks over here.

GERALD   Yes.

            (*Pause.*)

(GERALD)   Have they all gone?

TIMOTHY   From round here? Yes, thank God. Couldn't get home quick enough.

GERALD   Well, can hardly blame them.

TIMOTHY   Suppose not.

     (TIMOTHY *raises his glass . . .*)

     To survivors.

GERALD   To survivors!

     (*They both take a sip.*

     A flash of lightning.)

GERALD   One . . . two . . . three . . . four . . . five . . . six . . . seven . . . eight . . .

     (*Crack of thunder. Definitely further away now.*)

     Yes, much farther away.

TIMOTHY   Much.

GERALD   I must say, it's all rather odd though.

TIMOTHY   What is?

GERALD   That weather . . . almost . . . well, it's as if we were in a ghost story.

TIMOTHY   Yes.

GERALD   What with that séance and Zelma going into that trance.

TIMOTHY   I think it was a fit.

GERALD   Or fit, yes. And that bell ringing.

TIMOTHY	And you're certain . . .
GERALD	I promise you, I didn't touch it.
TIMOTHY	Or knock the table?
GERALD	Not me old boy, I assure you.
TIMOTHY	Nor me.
GERALD	I don't see Penny doing anything either, she plays with such a straight bat.
TIMOTHY	She does. She does. And Betsy . . .
GERALD	Poor girl was too terrified to move herself let alone a table or a bell!
TIMOTHY	Yes, that's true enough.
GERALD	You don't think you should pop up and see how she's getting along?
TIMOTHY	Hardly. Penny is much better at that business than me. And the Van Tanzen woman is up there . . . doing whatever she's meant to be doing.
GERALD	A protective charm she called it.
TIMOTHY	That's right. Completely barmy if you ask me.
GERALD	Do you think so?
TIMOTHY	Of course I do. I don't think for one moment any of us made the bell ring or the window slam shut or make those funny noises . . .
GERALD	No.
TIMOTHY	But I wouldn't put it past her.
GERALD	Who . . . Van Tanzen?

TIMOTHY	Would you?
GERALD	I really don't know, old boy. She's got a reputation to uphold.
TIMOTHY	Precisely. She can't afford to disappoint, can she?
GERALD	You mean to say, you think her a fraud?
TIMOTHY	A harmless fraud. But a fraud nonetheless. I'm hardly going to call the local bobby, am I? But yes, I reckon we've been had.
GERALD	I'm not too sure, you know.
TIMOTHY	Oh come on, Gerald, not you too? It's all nonsense.
GERALD	Then why did you invite her here?
TIMOTHY	For a bit of fun. And it was just that. Sadly it all got a little out of hand.
GERALD	Exactly. How can you say it's all harmless fun when your wife is up there shaking like a leaf and freezing cold, insisting that she saw a face at that window? Staring right at her. The face of evil itself.
	(*They both turn, solemnly, towards the window. The lights flicker.*)
TIMOTHY	(*Rising with purpose.*) Poppycock! It's all that Van Tanzen woman's doing. She's a gifted master of ceremonies, don't you see? What an act she put on from the moment she entered, whipping us all into a frenzy of make believe and eventually . . . hysteria. Goodness me! You know what Betsy's like . . . she's always been a bag of nerves. Good God man, I knocked over a china teacup the other day and she had to take herself to bed for the afternoon. The girl is

on edge, all the damn time. I love her, I really
do but she is easily affected by the smallest of
events. And this Van Tanzen . . . she's no fool.
She would have seen this and worked out that if
she created enough of an atmosphere and hit the
table at the right time when no one was looking,
well, she'd create a veritable storm of fear and
uncertainty. And it worked! We were, as the
Americans would say . . . 'suckers' for it all.

GERALD   Well, she seemed pretty shaken up to me. More
than usual.

TIMOTHY   You don't live with her.

GERALD   Still . . . she looked dreadful. As if she'd seen . . .

TIMOTHY   . . . A ghost?

GERALD   Well, yes actually.

TIMOTHY   Dear me, she's really done a job on us hasn't
she?

GERALD   And that trance, or fit or whatever we're going
to call it? There are actresses on the West End
who couldn't pull that performance off.

TIMOTHY   She's got talent, I'll give her that. But as you say,
her talent lies it mendacity and manipulation,
not in channelling the spirits of the dead.

GERALD   But here's the rub . . .

TIMOTHY   Oh, yes? Do go on.

GERALD   She said this chap's spirit was too strong, even
for her. That she didn't think she would be able
to rest his tortured soul.

TIMOTHY   And your point is?

GERALD   Well, if she really were a fraud why would she
              say that? Wouldn't it be better for her and her
              reputation if she were able to deal with this
              spirit and leave here a heroine in everybody's
              eyes?

TIMOTHY   She's still here isn't she? Upstairs casting her
              protective spell or whatever . . . she's dragging
              this out as long as possible. And mark my
              words, she may have refused any payment thus
              far but if I were to offer her some money by the
              end of the night I am certain she will take it.
              Oh yes, she knows what game she's playing and
              she's a master at it.

              (Pause.)

GERALD   I don't believe you.

TIMOTHY   You don't believe what?

GERALD   That you're as cynical as you're trying to make
              out. Of course I have my reservations but at
              least I am open minded about it.

TIMOTHY   I'm a solicitor. I am paid not to have an open
              mind.

GERALD   Nonsense. You're an intelligent, well-read and
              informed man. You may know how to deal in
              facts and what is proven but you also possess
              a mind sharp enough and clear enough to
              appreciate there are certain things that fall not
              under our sphere of understanding. Only a
              fool dismisses the potential of mystery and you
              Timothy, are no fool.

TIMOTHY   How kind.

GERALD   Now I'm not going to stand here and tell you
              that I believe in the supernatural nor that this
              evening has made me feel otherwise but I can

tell you with complete conviction, that I am at
the very least willing to consider the possibility
that this evening's events are, perhaps,
supernatural in some way shape or form.

TIMOTHY   Are you indeed?

GERALD   I am. And I believe you are too. You're just not
willing to admit it. Your whole attitude to this
evening's events are too clear-cut for my liking.
I think it's a defence strategy.

TIMOTHY   I have no idea what you're talking about.

GERALD   I remember my father telling me about a young
man he met in London one afternoon. He was
walking down Piccadilly, this was . . . two,
maybe three years after the Great War. And
this young man walked up to him as bright as a
button and in the middle of Piccadilly, saluted
my father. Now this young man had been in
the trenches with my father at the Somme.
Father couldn't remember him but he certainly
remembered my father. The young man shook
my father's hand and said he had always wanted
to ask him one question . . . the men in the
trenches were tired, cold, hungry and scared,
they were bloody terrified, of course they were.
But how, this young man asked my father, how
come he was never scared. My father leaned in
and told him that he wasn't as scared as any of
the men under him . . . he was more scared. He
had in his charge hundreds of young men like
him who could at any moment be killed. The
difference was, that when he looked into the
eyes of those young men and saw fear, they had
to look into his eyes and see the opposite. My
father wasn't allowed to be scared and he was
the master at pretending not to be.

TIMOTHY	I know what's coming. Your father got home and somehow discovered that the young man who had come up to him in Piccadilly was in fact dead and had died at the Somme . . . this is some sort of ghost story, yes?
GERALD	Quite wrong. The young man was alive and well. No, what I am getting at is that you are the host and the reason why Zelma Van Tanzen is here tonight. You don't want to but you believe everything that has happened and you're down right scared. Terrified in fact. You just can't allow yourself to show it.
TIMOTHY	What utter drivel!
GERALD	Is it?
TIMOTHY	Of course it is. There's absolutely nothing to be scared about.
GERALD	Then prove it.
TIMOTHY	Happily, although I don't know how.
GERALD	If you really don't think that there's anything odd about what's happened this evening or that something supernatural has occurred . . .
TIMOTHY	Yes?
GERALD	Then ring the bell.
	(*Pause.*)
	You know what Zelma said before she went upstairs with the girls.
TIMOTHY	(*dismissively*) I can't remember.
GERALD	She said . . . leave the bell on the table and alert her the moment it rings.

TIMOTHY   Oh, that's right.

GERALD   And she also said, on no account should we
               ring the bell ourselves for that would act as
               an invitation to the spirit to enter and walk
               amongst us.

               (*Beat.*)

GERALD   You remember don't you?

TIMOTHY   I suppose so.

GERALD   Well then, if it really is nonsense . . . ring the
               bell.

               (*Pause.*)

TIMOTHY   I have nothing to prove to you.

GERALD   I knew it! I knew you couldn't do it.

TIMOTHY   You do it then!

GERALD   No thank you very much, I'm willing to admit
               that I don't want to toy with such things. You
               were the one who called it poppycock.

TIMOTHY   Well it is poppycock.

GERALD   Just admit it, you're as scared as me. Why, I
               think you're worse. You're as scared as dear
               Betsy upstairs.

TIMOTHY   You're being awfully childish, Gerald.

GERALD   I just like being proved right.

TIMOTHY   You're not right.

GERALD   And yet, Your Honour, we have no evidence to
               the contrary.

(Pause.)

TIMOTHY   Fine! Fine . . . if it'll shut you up, I'll ring the
                  damned bell!

                  (TIMOTHY *approaches the bell; his hand wavers*
                  above it as he prepares himself to pick it up.
                  He looks at GERALD. TIMOTHY *picks up the bell*
                  carefully, takes a deep but surreptitious breath
                  and rings the bell.

                  Silence.)

                  See . . . poppycock.

                  (*Suddenly a piercing scream comes from*
                  upstairs. It is BETSY.)

TIMOTHY   Betsy?

                  (*He rushes to the foot of the stairs but his path*
                  is blocked by ZELMA *who flies down the stairs.*)

ZELMA   Who rang the bell?

TIMOTHY   What the hell happened? Betsy!

ZELMA   She's as safe as she can be . . . although I don't
                  know for how long.

TIMOTHY   (*trying to go upstairs but he is blocked by* ZELMA)
                  I must see her.

ZELMA   There is nothing you can do, trust me.

GERALD   And Penelope . . . where's she?

ZELMA   With Betsy, quite safe.

GERALD   And I have to take your word for that, do I?

ZELMA   Who else's word will you take? Trust me,
                  gentlemen, I have applied a protective charm to

Betsy but if either of you go upstairs, his anger will increase and you shall be placing your lives and the lives of your spouses in mortal danger.

MICHAEL   (*From circle level of auditorium.*) That's not the line!

DIANA   Who said that . . . ?

HUGO   Our maestro.

               (DIANA *shields her eyes from the stage lights.*)

DIANA   I can't see a bloody thing. Hello! Hello! If you're going to interrupt me in full flow, at least have the decency to show yourself.

MICHAEL   For God's sake . . . I am up here! UP HERE!

DIANA   Oh, there you are. Clive . . . are these lights correct, they seem awfully low?

CLIVE   (*Next to or near to* MICHAEL.) That's what Michael asked for.

DIANA   Michael?

MICHAEL   The lights are the least of our sodding problems. Right now I am more interested in you getting your lines right.

               (SOPHIE *and* ALISON *appear from the wings, chatting happily.*)

MICHAEL   I'm sorry, is this rehearsal interrupting your conversation? Please, carry on.

ALISON   Oh, sorry . . . I thought we'd stopped.

MICHAEL   Yes! We have stopped . . . we've come to a great big fucking stop but that doesn't mean you

	two can saunter onto the stage as if you're out for a walk in the park!
Hugo	Trust me, no one thinks this is a walk in the park.
Michael	I'm sorry, Hugo? Would you mind repeating that?
Hugo	Doesn't matter.
Michael	So keep your mouths shut whilst mine is open. Diana, you went wrong.
Diana	Story of my life, dear.
Michael	With the line . . . with your sodding line!
Diana	Did I?
Michael	You said . . . "placing the lives of your spouses in mortal danger."
Diana	I did.
Michael	That is wrong!
Diana	That's a matter of opinion.
Michael	No, it's a matter of the script! Words on a page!
Diana	And the words on the page say "placing the lives of your wives in mortal danger." Now I know I'm not Alan Bennett but even I can tell that that line is utter shit. Hence my changing it.
Michael	Say the lines as they are on the page.
Diana	Even if they are total shit?
Michael	Even if they are total shit. I want this play word for word. It is a revival, not a reworking. From Gerald . . . "And I have to take your word for it do I?" Anyone not meant to be on stage, fuck off.

(*The actors take their places where they left off.* ALISON *and* SOPHIE *pick up their conversation where they left off and saunter towards the wings.*)

MICHAEL   Alison, Sophie! Other side, please!

SOPHIE   Oh, yes!

             (*They giggle as they head the other way.*)

MICHAEL   What the hell are you doing?

ALISON   We're fucking off!

MICHAEL   Then do it faster!

             (*They pick up pace and exit.*)

             Right . . . go ahead, please.

GERALD   And I have to take your word for that, do I?

ZELMA   Who else's word will you take? Trust me, gentlemen, I have applied a protective charm to Betsy but if either of you go upstairs, his anger will increase and you shall be placing your lives and the lives of your wives in mortal danger.

EDDIE   [*Corpses.*]

DIANA   Don't . . . please.

MICHAEL   Again!

GERALD   (*Although* EDDIE *is struggling not to laugh.*) And I have to take your word for that, do I?

ZELMA   (*Also struggling.*) Who else's word will you take? Trust me, gentlemen, I have applied a protective charm to Betsy but if either of you go upstairs, his anger will increase and you shall be placing

	your lives and . . . the lives of your wives in mortal danger.
	(*Now joined by* HUGO, *they all descend into fits of giggles.*)
DIANA	I'm sorry . . . I'm sorry . . . I just . . .
HUGO	Maybe we should protect the lives or our wives with some knives!
	(*They all crack up, uncontrollably.*)
MICHAEL	If we weren't opening tomorrow night, so help me God I would fire you on the spot right now.
CLIVE	(*Shouting across.*) I think we may all be a little tired.
MICHAEL	Oh, do you, Clive? How very compassionate of you. Not to mention insightful . . . who would have thought we'd all be tired and wrung out and going absolutely bloody mental! Of course we are. I haven't slept properly in weeks but do you see me cackling like a demented hyena?
DIANA	(*Recovering from her hysterics.*) If only you would . . .
MICHAEL	And what's that meant to mean?
	(SOPHIE *and* ALISON *enter from the wings again.*)
SOPHIE	I didn't get it. What's so funny?
DIANA	Oh bloody hell.
MICHAEL	I'm coming down.
ALISON	I think Clive's right, we're all a bit overtired. We should take a break.

EDDIE   I thought the scene was going rather well?

HUGO   It was, wonderfully well.

EDDIE   He's rather obsessed with us getting this play
                 word perfect isn't he?

HUGO   He is obsessed, that's the problem. Totally
                 obsessed with the whole damn play.

CLIVE   (*Shouting down.*) I thought it looked great, guys.

                 (*They mumble thanks to* CLIVE.

                 The GHOST *appears in the auditorium.*

                 During this, SOPHIE *has walked to the edge of
                 the stage and is staring into the auditorium as if
                 she's seen something.*)

ALISON   Sophie? Is everything all right?

                 (*Beat.*)

                 Sophie, what is it?

SOPHIE   Mm? Oh, nothing. I thought I saw someone in
                 the auditorium, that's all.

                 (*The* GHOST *leaves.*)

ALISON   It'll be Michael, won't it?

SOPHIE   No, I don't think so.

ALISON   Michael? Is that you?

                 (MICHAEL *enters from the other side of the stalls.*)

MICHAEL   Is what me?

ALISON   Oh, you're there.

MICHAEL   I am. Unfortunately.

SOPHIE   It was probably just the lights.

MICHAEL   (*Making his way onto stage.*) Gather round.

ALISON   It's all this talk of ghosts and such. We're all a
               little on edge.

SOPHIE   I think you're right.

EDDIE   (*Catching the end of their conversation.*) If
               you want a little help with how to deal with
               opening-night nerves, you and I can go to my
               dressing room . . . I have a wonderful breathing
               technique I could teach you.

               (SOPHIE *smiles politely.*)

DIANA   I bet you do.

MICHAEL   She doesn't have time to be taught breathing
               techniques, thank you, Eddie. Sophie, we're
               going to do your monologue just before the
               spirit cabinet scene, yes?

SOPHIE   Oh, right. We're not carrying on from where we
               left off?

MICHAEL   No. I fear we shall descend into further
               madness if we do that. We'll move on. That
               scene looks in okay shape as it happens, well
               done boys.

HUGO   Bloody hell! Is that a compliment, Michael my
               dear?

MICHAEL   It would appear so. Look . . . I know we're all
               tired, but there are few areas we need to tidy
               up. Sophie . . .

DIANA   Yes, that's one area.

MICHAEL   (*Ignoring this.*) . . . Sophie, my sweet, we'll do
                 your monologue and then we'll move onto the
                 spirit cabinet scene. Clive?

CLIVE   (*From up above still.*) Yes boss?

MICHAEL   We'll be doing the spirit cabinet scene after
                 I've done some one-on-one with Sophie for
                 her monologue . . . (*This causes childish glee
                 between the other cast members.*) We all set to
                 go on that?

CLIVE   I'll come down and sort the props out, but yep
                 we'll be ready.

                 (CLIVE *begins to make his way down from the
                 circle.*)

MICHAEL   Excellent. Right, the rest of you can take a
                 break. Have a coffee, a bite, a fag . . .

DIANA   . . . Thank God!

MICHAEL   . . . And I'll make sure Clive gives you a call
                 when you're needed back up here, okay?

                 (*They all mumble their acknowledgements and
                 begin to leave the stage. As they walk off . . .*)

ALISON   I'll be mother.

EDDIE   Lovely. Tea please, darling.

HUGO   Coffee.

ALISON   White with one?

HUGO   Please.

DIANA   Coffee. As dark as hell and as heavy as treacle.
                 Bring it to stage door will you? I'll be outside.
                 (*She mimes puffing on a cigarette.*)

(*They all leave the stage leaving only* Michael *and* Sophie, *who have been going through her monologue from his script. She nods and smiles but is evidently confused.*)

Michael   Does that make sense?

Sophie   I think so.

Michael   Vulnerability, that's the key.

Sophie   Vulnerability, sure.

Michael   And learning the lines.

Sophie   Got it.

Michael   This is an opportunity for the audience to see Betsy as an attractive but flawed, cursed even . . . young woman. She is in a marriage that is not making her entirely happy in a house that frankly terrifies her. She's timid and feels very alone.

Sophie   Yes . . . alone. I get that, I understand that.

Michael   There's a real danger with Betsy that she can become very . . . wet. And wet is annoying. Annoying characters don't sell. Right?

Sophie   Right.

Michael   So what I want from you, and we've talked about this before, haven't we? What I want from you is a delicacy of touch, an awareness of imperfections, living contradictions. Heavy and cursed and yet floating . . . and . . . soufflé-like.

Sophie   Soufflé?

Michael   Exactly.

SOPHIE	As in the omelette?
MICHAEL	–
	(*Beat.*)
	Let's just give it a go, should we?
	(MICHAEL *goes to stand in the corner of the stage and watch* . . .)
	(SOPHIE *walks to the centre of the stage* . . .)
SOPHIE	Erm . . .
MICHAEL	What?
SOPHIE	There's no one else on stage at this moment?
MICHAEL	That's right. This is just Betsy, talking to the spirit. Pleading, communicating.
	(SOPHIE *sits down* . . .)
SOPHIE	I think I'm sitting, right?
MICHAEL	I believe so.
SOPHIE	And then I get up on the first line?
MICHAEL	Just do what comes naturally. I'm not worried about the blocking. I'm worried about the lines. Very worried about the lines.
SOPHIE	Sure.
MICHAEL	Remember . . . heavy soufflé.
SOPHIE	Uh huh.
	(*Pause.*
	SOPHIE *steadies herself.*)

BETSY   Hello? Hello? Can you hear me? Oh, I really
                 don't know. Perhaps this is madness. Yes,
                 that's exactly what it is. Madness. I have lost
                 my mind, surely. How else can I explain the
                 feelings that have overtaken me this evening?
                 The shadow of ice that has seemingly possessed
                 my spirit since the séance. Such things, they are
                 beyond our understanding of the natural order
                 of the world. Even as a woman I understand
                 that there are realms in this universe as
                 yet undiscovered and untouched by man's
                 endeavour. And these realms hold within their
                 midst the shadow of death itself and the hollow
                 echo of the restless dead. But do I believe or
                 was I, as Timothy thinks, simply the victim
                 of some sort of hysteria? I am, I must admit,
                 susceptible to such things. And yet, this feeling
                 of being haunted refuses to leave me.

                 (*Pause. She shivers.*)

                 Who was that I saw at the window? Was it you?
                 Really you? If you can hear me, give me a sign.

                 (*Beat.*)

SOPHIE   Don't we have bumps there or something?

MICHAEL   Yes . . . well, the bell rings.

SOPHIE   That's right, the bell rings.

                 (*She looks expectantly at* MICHAEL.)

MICHAEL   Oh, okay . . . no worries.

                 (MICHAEL *picks up the bell. Is there the slightest
                 sense of trepidation on his part?*)

BETSY   Who was that I saw at the window? Was it you?
                 Really you? If you can hear me, give me a sign.

(MICHAEL *rings the bell.*)

BETSY

(*With a sharp intake of breath*) Yes! You are here. I can feel you.

(*The ghost of* ALDERWICK HAYE *appears somewhere subtle but noticeable.*)

I ask you to leave me be. I am not your wife, your poor departed wife. I cannot begin to comprehend the pain you felt, the anguish you must surely still endure. You have my sympathy. But if Miss Van Tanzen is correct in her thinking, you have come to take my soul with you. As what? An act of revenge? I am not your wife, I cannot comfort you.

(*Pause.*

The GHOST *leaves.*)

SOPHIE

Shit! I'm sorry . . .

MICHAEL

What?

SOPHIE

It's gone.

MICHAEL

You were doing so well, you really were. Here . . .

(*He puts the bell down before going over and handing her the script to read.*)

You remember now?

SOPHIE

Yes, I think so. I am so sorry.

(*He puts his arm around her.*)

MICHAEL

It was terrific. You're a star in the making.

SOPHIE

You really think so?

MICHAEL

I do.

SOPHIE   I often wonder why you offered me this part . . .
                       I mean . . . I am so grateful, don't get me wrong
                       but I know the others laugh at me and Diana
                       positively hates me.

MICHAEL   Diana positively hates everyone. And the others
                       aren't laughing at you. We work within a small
                       world and those who try to infiltrate that world
                       are often teased at first but trust me, once
                       you have delivered this performance they will
                       welcome you happily as one of their own. We
                       are a fickle bunch who can turn from hate to
                       love at the drop of a curtain.

SOPHIE   Thank you.

                       (*A moment between them.*)

                       Diana says you only hired me because I am
                       a cheap American. Because if you have an
                       American in the cast you get more coverage . . .
                       opportunities for investment and more chance
                       of a Broadway transfer.

MICHAEL   That's just Diana's unwavering cynicism.
                       Remember, Diana was once as pretty and as
                       young as you. And she positively hates you for
                       that.

SOPHIE   Because I'm young?

MICHAEL   Worse. Because you'll upstage her.

                       (*They smile together. The lights flicker.*)

                       Right. Why don't I go and make us both
                       a coffee? You have a look over the script,
                       reacquaint yourself with the lines and I'll be
                       back in five minutes to go over it again, yes?

SOPHIE   That sounds like a good idea.

MICHAEL   Great.

                (*As he leaves . . .*)

                Have some fun with it whilst I'm not here. You
                have the whole theatre to yourself. No one is
                watching. Speak the lines to everyone and no
                one. Enjoy it. You're all alone.

                (*He exits, not before he throws a glance into
                the auditorium . . . has he seen something? He
                looks back at* SOPHIE *who is now engrossed in
                the script and is mouthing the words to herself.*

                Exits.)

SOPHIE   Everyone and no one. Here goes nothing.

                (*She steals a glance at the script . . .*)

                You are fuelled by anger and hatred. Hatred
                of wandering this earth with such pain in your
                soul. But the taking of my soul will surely not
                placate your fury.

                (*Pause.*)

                Show yourself! Have the bravery to show
                yourself instead of cowering in the shadows. If
                you insist on making me a victim –

                (*She stops. She has seen something in the
                auditorium.*)

SOPHIE   Hello? Clive, is that you.

                (*The lights flicker. The bell rings.*)

                Hello . . . ?

(*Tapping, getting closer and closer and louder and louder. Suddenly it stops at the loudest point that we have heard it thus far.*

Only SOPHIE'S *panicked breath is heard.*

Then, almost imperceptibly, the face of ALDERWICK HAYE *appears at the window. It emerges from the shadows as the veritable face of death. Although we find it difficult to distinguish features, we are in no doubt that this face is a face of evil, hatred and pain. Hollow and white.*

SOPHIE *doesn't see the* GHOST.

The face disappears into the blackness. SOPHIE *steadies herself and begins her lines again.*)

SOPHIE   Clive? Hugo? If this is some kind of joke . . . grow up. Right? Right?

                 (*Pause. She takes a breath and looks again at the script before . . .*)

BETSY   You are fuelled by anger and hatred. Hatred of wandering this earth with such pain in your soul. But the taking of my soul will surely not placate your fury.

                 (*A knock at the door.*)

SOPHIE   Hugo . . . I know that's you. Stop it!

                 (*Another knock.*

                 She starts to make her way to the door, very slowly, terrified.

                 The door begins the rattle, growing in violence and energy. Suddenly it stops. Summoning whatever bravery she can muster, SOPHIE *puts*

*her hand on the doorknob and throws the door
open. No one is there.*

*The bell rings more violently than ever before.
The lights flicker more violently than before.
In her terrified confusion,* SOPHIE *backs away
towards the door. The lights snap the blackout.*

Silence.

*Suddenly, with a harrowing noise (a cross
between a male scream and a loud moan) the
face of* ALDERWICK HAYE *appears behind her in
the doorframe – he is bearing down upon her.
She screams and runs but she can't find her
way. The face disappears as she stumbles over
the furniture, makes it to the other side of the
stage.* CLIVE *leaps out from the wings, giving
her a huge shock. The lights come back on. He
holds her as she weeps with fear in his arms.*

CLIVE   Here, here. Calm down, calm down. You're all
                   right.

SOPHIE   He's here, he's actually here.

                   (MICHAEL *comes running in.*)

MICHAEL   What the hell happened? Sophie . . . are you all
                   right?

CLIVE   I think I gave her a bit of a shock.

                   (CLIVE *helps her to the settee and throws a look
                   at* MICHAEL *that suggests he thinks she's off her
                   rocker.*)

SOPHIE   No, no it wasn't you. It was him. He's here. I
                   know he is.

MICHAEL   Who's here, sweetheart?

SOPHIE	The ghost . . . that man was right. We've awoken him and he's back.
MICHAEL	You mean . . . Alderwick Haye?
SOPHIE	Yes. He's here.
MICHAEL	Now, come on Sophie . . . you don't mean to tell me that you believe in that. It's an old wives' tale, nothing more.
SOPHIE	(*Leaping up.*) It is more, it's much, much more. I saw him. I saw his face.
MICHAEL	(*Helping her back into the settee.*) Okay, okay. Just relax, try to calm down. Clive, did you see anything?
CLIVE	Afraid not . . . I was in the props room getting the spirit cabinet ready. I was just coming back onto the stage when she ran right into me.
SOPHIE	But the lights . . . you must have noticed that the lights were off?
CLIVE	Suppose so, but they are a little dicky . . . I'm going to have to do some work on them overnight, I'm afraid.
SOPHIE	No! The lights aren't broken . . . it's him. You should have seen his face. He was evil, pure evil.

(MICHAEL *and* CLIVE *stare at one another and then into the auditorium.*)

And the worst thing was . . . I felt him . . . He was actually coming for me. I could feel it . . . he was after me.

(*The rest of the cast appear from the wings.*)

HUGO	What's wrong . . . Sophie. Are you okay?
MICHAEL	She's fine, she's had a bit of a shock.
DIANA	(*Reading the newspaper.*) What, she actually remembered her lines this time?
MICHAEL	Don't be a bitch, Diana. The girl's on edge.
SOPHIE	I saw him. I saw Alderwick Haye.
ALISON	I knew it. I knew we shouldn't have been messing about with this stuff . . . we don't know what we're dealing with.
MICHAEL	We're dealing with a play! That's all. Sophie is under a lot of stress, not helped by some of you and your attitude towards her! The poor girl is at the end of her tether and her mind is playing tricks.
SOPHIE	I am not insane! I know what I saw.
ALISON	I believe you, darling.
	(ALISON *sits down next to her on the sofa to comfort her.*)
MICHAEL	This is ridiculous. That idiot Professor has a lot to answer for, coming in here and planting hogwash stories in our heads.
ALISON	Professor Heath did say if we did the entire séance scene . . .
MICHAEL	Professor Heath is a madman.
ALISON	All I'm saying is that we did do the entire scene.
MICHAEL	Of course we did, it's in the bloody play!
EDDIE	And Diana did have a funny turn.

DIANA   (*Looking up from her newspaper.*) That's
                because I hadn't had a fag for an hour!

ALISON   You're saying you're not in the least bit
                concerned about tonight's events? You don't
                even feel the slightest sense of fear?

DIANA   Of course . . . I'm terrified that my agent will
                see me in this!

ALISON   Be serious for once, Diana!

                (*Pause.*)

DIANA   (*Putting newspaper down.*) Fine. All right, if you
                must know, I do feel a little odd. God knows
                what happened to me during that scene. But I'm
                a realist, I apply good old-fashioned logic and,
                most importantly, I'm a professional! I get on
                with what I am paid to do.

MICHAEL   Bravo!

DIANA   But to be quite honest, I don't feel right about
                this. Any of it. What if we are playing with
                something we should be leaving alone . . .

MICHAEL   Not you as well?

DIANA   It's worth considering, that's all.

MICHAEL   No it's not!

ALISON   I think perhaps we should go home. All get
                some sleep and come back in the morning and
                see how we feel then.

EDDIE   Not a bad idea.

HUGO   (*Checking his watch.*) May catch last orders.

MICHAEL	Like hell! We still have the majority of the second half to get through. We open tomorrow night! We can't afford to go home and 'get some sleep'.
EDDIE	You can't expect Sophie to rehearse, look at her.
MICHAEL	Sophie is fine, aren't you?
SOPHIE	Erm . . .
MICHAEL	Of course she is! Diana . . . ?
DIANA	Always the professional.
MICHAEL	Exactly! Now we've all had a break, all I want to do is finish off the trickier parts of the second half and then you can all bugger off and get some sleep, okay?
ALISON	Trickier parts?
MICHAEL	Yes . . . we all set, Clive?
CLIVE	All set.
ALISON	You mean the spirit cabinet scene?
MICHAEL	I do.
EDDIE	Do you think that's wise, what with all that's gone on?
MICHAEL	I think it's exactly what needs to be done. To prove that all this nonsense you all seem to suddenly buy into is exactly that . . . complete rubbish. Clive . . . bring it on please. The rest of you get yourselves together.

(*They all seem rather reluctant.*)

Look! We're going to do this either way so the
sooner we do the sooner we get to go. It's up to
you.

(*They all get up and move.* DIANA *chucks her
newspaper into the wings,* CLIVE *exits. General
chatter and movement.* SOPHIE *and* ALISON *chat
earnestly . . .*)

ALISON   Are you sure you're going to be all right?

SOPHIE   I'll be fine, thank you. You're always so kind to
                me.

ALISON   This play, it means a great deal to Michael. He
                needs it to be a success. People are saying he's
                past it, that he'll never direct another hit again.
                I think that's why he's behaving as he is. I've
                never seen him like this before.

SOPHIE   He's just passionate, I guess.

ALISON   Yes. Yes, he's passionate all right.

MICHAEL   CLIVE!

CLIVE   (*Off.*) Coming!

                (CLIVE *enters, wheeling a spirit cabinet with red
                velvet curtain. He throws two lengths of rope
                on the table as he passes. Then he places the
                spirit cabinet centre stage and locks the wheels.
                He places one of the chairs from the table
                inside the cabinet and places the spirit bell on
                the floor beside the chair.*)

CLIVE   That okay?

MICHAEL   Fine. You'll have to get in quicker than that on
                the night, I want the scene change to be super
                fast.

CLIVE	(*Through gritted teeth.*) I'll make sure to rehearse.
MICHAEL	Do. Right!
	(*He claps his hands together.*)
	All ready?
	(*Mumbled acknowledgements of readiness.*)
	Good! We'll go from where Betsy is tied up. Full energy please!
	(MICHAEL *goes into the auditorium. The others gather in their positions.*)
CLIVE	I'll run up and sort out the lights.
	(*He runs off through the auditorium.*)
MICHAEL	Whilst we're waiting, we may as well get on with it.
	(ZELMA *stands centre stage as the others watch her intensely.*)
ZELMA	Ladies and Gentlemen, I shall soon be asking you to tie Mrs Grey's hands and legs. This is as much for her safety as it is for yours. Once the spirit takes hold I anticipate the strength to be greater than any I have encountered before.
GERALD	I say, is this quite safe?
TIMOTHY	Of course it is, it's a party trick.
PENELOPE	Don't be rude, Timothy.
ZELMA	I assure you it is no party trick and as for the safety, I cannot be sure. All I know is that if we wish to placate this restless spirit who is

intent on taking the soul of Mrs Grey, this is a measure most necessary. Now, once the curtain is closed you will hear the bell ring and you may hear Mrs Grey groan and wail . . . do not be alarmed, this is all part of the channelling process. Once we have the spirit in the room with us we can ascertain how to deliver him to peace.

BETSY   And how exactly are we to do that?

ZELMA   I shall engage the spirit?

GERALD   Engage?

ZELMA   Converse.

TIMOTHY   Small talk with a spirit, eh?

ZELMA   (With ferocity.) This is no joke, Mr Grey! There is no reason for revelry or lightness of heart. Your wife's very soul is at stake!

TIMOTHY   Well . . . I'm . . . I'm terribly sorry, I am sure. Please carry on.

ZELMA   Mrs Grey . . . are you quite ready?

BETSY   Yes, I suppose so.

ZELMA   Gentlemen, the rope please.

(TIMOTHY and GERALD take a length of rope each from the table. BETSY is escorted into the spirit cabinet by ZELMA who sits her down onto the chair. The men tie up her legs and arms.)

Make sure the ties are quite secure. Mrs Grey?

BETSY   Yes, they're secure.

ZELMA   Excellent.

(*The lights dim.*

And so we begin.

ZELMA *closes the curtains around the spirit cabinet.*)

Gentlemen, please stand away from the cabinet.

(*The men move to the sides of the room.* PENELOPE *joins her husband.*)

GERALD   I must say, I am not too sure about this.

PENELOPE   No, but one assumes she knows what she's doing.

(ZELMA *takes a deep breath and prepares herself.*)

ZELMA   No interruptions please, whatever happens I shall be the judge on when to end proceedings.

(*Pause.*)

Oh, most-respected spirit. We know you have joined us, we know you walk among us now. Come forth and alert us to your presence.

(*Pause.*

The bell rings.)

You are most welcome and we ask you to remain with us as we work together to assist you in your quest for peace.

(*The bell rings, more violently.*

DIANA *looks up to the box, confused.*)

MICHAEL   Stay in the moment!

ZELMA   We require you to find peace and we ask that
                   we may be granted control over your spirit that
                   we may guide you to the light and to eternal
                   rest.

                   (Pause. This isn't meant to happen. DIANA looks
                   at ALISON who, equally confused, motions for
                   her to carry on regardless. She repeats . . .)

ZELMA   We require you to find peace and we ask that we
                   may be granted control over your spirit that we
                   may guide you to the light and to eternal rest.

                   (Pause.)

                   Eternal rest! God damn it!! That's the damn cue!!

                   (The bell rings and rings and rings, louder and
                   louder until it flies out over the spirit cabinet
                   and lands on the floor.)

DIANA   What the bloody hell . . . ?

MICHAEL   Carry on!

ALISON   Are you joking?

MICHAEL   It's good . . . I like it. Come on, get on with it!

ZELMA   I am here to be your guide, your hope and your
                   deliverer of peace. Trust me as we trust in you
                   to do Mrs Grey no harm.

                   (We hear the chair in the cabinet thud up and
                   down upon the floor, as if SOPHIE is moving
                   erratically.)

HUGO   You could have told us you'd made a few
                   changes!

MICHAEL   Just shut up!

ZELMA   No harm must be done to Mrs Grey! You must
                 leave this house and its occupants in peace. No
                 sanctuary can be found through the destruction
                 of others in this realm or the next. You must
                 find the light and allow me to escort you there.

                 (*The chair gets louder and louder. It stops.*
                 SOPHIE *screams. The lights go out through the*
                 entire theatre.)

HUGO   What the bloody hell is going on?

ALISON   Sophie? Are you all right?

EDDIE   Michael? What is this? Clive?

DIANA   Shhh!

                 (*Silence.*

                 The door opens slowly.

                 We hear the disembodied voice as before . . .)

VOICE   No peace.

                 (*Door slams shut.*

                 A member of the audience (planted actor who
                 plays CLIVE *or* GILES) *suddenly jumps up . . .*)

AUDIENCE
MEMBER   What the bloody hell is that? (*Or similar.*)

                 (*Audience are allowed to react!*

                 The spirit cabinet begins to shake.)

SOPHIE   He's here! He's here!

EDDIE   Sophie!

(EDDIE *runs towards the spirit cabinet but
something throws him back.* HUGO *runs over to
help him.*)

SOPHIE   Help! Help me!

                  (*A final scream and the spirit cabinet stops
                  shaking.*

                  After a moment EDDIE *gets back up and
                  tentatively approaches the spirit cabinet. He
                  summons the courage and throws the curtain
                  back.*)

ALISON   (*As he does this.*) Eddie, no!

                  (SOPHIE *has gone. The chair is on its side.*)

HUGO   Where is she?

                  (*Then, from the depths of the theatre we hear*
                  SOPHIE *scream.*)

EDDIE   Sophie!

                  (EDDIE *runs up to the door and the ghost of*
                  ALDERWICK HAYE *appears in the doorframe.* EDDIE
                  *wails in fear and falls back. The door slams shut
                  and the lights come back on.*)

ALISON   Michael? Michael? Where the hell has he gone?

HUGO   I don't mean to sound harsh, but I couldn't give
                  a shit. This play is over and I'm not staying here
                  a minute longer than I need to.

DIANA   Here, here.

EDDIE   We can't just leave Sophie . . .

ALISON   He's right . . . we need to stay and find her.

MICHAEL	(*Appearing from somewhere suitable.*) You won't find her. Not now.
ALISON	Michael, where the hell have you been?
EDDIE	What do you mean we won't find her?
MICHAEL	Because he's taken her. We were warned . . . and I didn't listen. I'm a fool. But he did come back. The play . . . brought him back.
HUGO	Alderwick Haye?
MICHAEL	And he's taken her.
EDDIE	Shit . . . I mean . . . why . . .
MICHAEL	Because it was written that way . . . she was always meant to be the one taken. (*Pause.*) (MICHAEL *sits, a shadow of his former self. Wide-eyed and terrified.*)
EDDIE	(*Attacking him and grabbing him.*) Then you're a damned fool!
HUGO	(*Pulling him off.*) Calm down! That's not going to do any good! (HUGO *manages to calm him down.*)
EDDIE	She's dead, isn't she? That's what you mean, she'd dead.
MICHAEL	Worse than dead.
EDDIE	So we'll call the police, you'll have to answer to them.
MICHAEL	Don't be an idiot. And tell them what? Well Officer . . . a member of our cast has been

dragged to hell by the vengeful spirit of a
former actor manager? We'll all be banged up
but in an asylum.

ALISON   But you're responsible.

MICHAEL   Fine, okay. I'm responsible. Go ahead, phone
the police. But I'll ask them what I'll ask you.
Prove it.

EDDIE   You're a selfish, egotistical madman. Look
where your bloody . . . vanity project has got
you . . .

(*He goes for him again. Again,* HUGO *is there to
hold him back.*)

Well, so much for saving your career. You'll
never work again.

HUGO   Come on, I for one don't want to hang around
here any longer than I need to.

(CLIVE *nods.*

EDDIE, CLIVE *and* HUGO *exit, followed closely
by* ALISON *who lingers a little longer in sheer
disbelief.*)

DIANA   Some things, Michael dearest . . . are meant to
be lost. Only a fool goes to find them.

(DIANA *exits.*

*After a moment, making sure that they have
gone,* MICHAEL *gets up and stands centre stage.
His face breaks into a grin, the grin into a smile
and the smile into a laugh.*)

MICHAEL   You're at rest now! I gave you what you asked
for . . . Exactly what you asked for!

(*The door to the auditorium flies open.* GILES HEATH *enters . . .*)

GILES   Oh no! No, no, no! I'm too late, aren't I?

MICHAEL   For what, Professor?

GILES   (*Making his way onto stage.*) I know . . . I worked it out! I worked out your sick game.

MICHAEL   Go on.

           (GILES *whips out an old photograph from his pocket.*)

GILES   Here!

MICHAEL   What am I looking at?

GILES   A photograph of the original acting company of this theatre. In the middle is Alderwick Haye and here . . . look! After I left this evening I couldn't get it out of my head, the American girl, I thought I knew her but for the life of me I couldn't place her. And then it struck me . . . I hadn't seen her before but I had seen someone who looks very much like her. (*Pointing at the photo again.*) A striking resemblance don't you think?

MICHAEL   Striking, indeed.

GILES   I found this photo when doing my research into Alderwick Haye. This was taken before they were married but that is Rose Blarney. Is it not?

MICHAEL   (*Superciliously.*) You tell me, you're the academic.

GILES   Don't play the fool with me you arrogant shit! You've played dumb all this time but you know

more about Alderwick Haye and this theatre
than me! How long did it take you to find her?

MICHAEL   I don't know who you're talking about?

GILES   Her great-great granddaughter!

MICHAEL   Oh, I see. Well, once I had heard the story
               of *Scared to Death* and the hearsay that
               surrounded it, I knew I had to see if it was true.
               What a play! What an opportunity . . . it was . . .
               is going to make me rich. It was easy enough
               to discover that Rose Blarney married again
               after Alderwick Haye's suicide. During a visit
               to the USA, she and her new husband decided
               to stay and raise a family. Dear Sophie, the girl
               who bears such a striking resemblance to her
               great-great grandmother was easy enough to
               trace once I had access to birth records. She
               was working as a secretary, bored out of her
               skull, so it was easy for me to engineer meeting
               her and wooing her with the chance of stardom
               over here in the UK. You know what, she even
               mentioned that she seemed to recollect a
               distant relative being in the theatre! God, she
               didn't inherit any of those genes however . . .
               she may look like Rose Blarney but she sure as
               hell couldn't act!

GILES   All this just to resurrect an old, lost play?

MICHAEL   Don't you get it?! It's easy to make a deal with
               the devil when you've got something to bargain
               with.

GILES   His wife's last remaining relative.

MICHAEL   Not only that but a relative that could be her
               in almost every way. He haunted this theatre
               because he wanted his wife back. He's now got
               her . . . he will leave my theatre in peace.

GILES   Your theatre?

MICHAEL   That's right. I have bought it. Meet the new
                 artistic director. The loan I had to take out will
                 be paid off within a year once *Scared to Death*
                 opens. No more curse, no more haunting. Just
                 a great play that no one has had the guts to
                 perform. Until now. We open in a month . . .
                 the cast, the real cast that is, arrive next week
                 to begin rehearsals. It's going to take the world
                 by storm. For years the entire industry has been
                 laughing at me, calling me 'past it' and a 'has
                 been'. No more. *Scared to Death* by Lucian
                 O'Keefe premieres in my own theatre in one
                 month.

GILES   You're mad.

MICHAEL   I'm ambitious. Now get out of my theatre and I
                 don't ever want to see you here again.

GILES   You'll pay. Somehow you'll pay.

                 (GILES *makes his way through the auditorium.*)

MICHAEL   You can't stop me Professor! Just like Eddie,
                 or Alison or Hugo . . . all we have is a missing
                 young lady. What's there to connect her
                 disappearance to me?

GILES   Oh, there's something. There's Alderwick Haye.

MICHAEL   Meaning?

GILES   Meaning, you may have made a deal with the
                 Devil . . . but he's still the Devil. And to him . . .
                 this theatre will never be yours. Goodnight.

                 (GILES *exits.*

                 Silence.

Tapping. Louder and louder and louder. It stops.

The spirit bell rings.)

MICHAEL   No! No . . . we had a deal. You've gone! WE HAD A DEAL!!

(*The bell stops ringing.*

The lights snap to blackout.

MICHAEL *runs.*

With the same hideous moan as before, ALDERWICK HAYE *appears.*

CURTAIN.)

Author's Note

To add to the verisimilitude and if your budget and indeed your fancy stretches, I suggest in the foyer of the theatre a fake bust of *Alderwick Haye* is presented. It should have no real attention drawn to it; it should simply look like many a bust in many a theatre foyer. Indeed, what would be marvellous would be to go as far as having posters for *Scared to Death* by Lucian O'Keefe on the walls rather than for *The Revival* by James Cawood. Admittedly, this may cause much consternation within the audience on arrival but nothing that a well-prepped Front of House and Box Office Staff won't be able to deal with!

I have also written the play in such a way that the Ghost can be played by the actors playing *Clive* and *Giles Heath* at different times. This requires an awareness of the actors' physical similarities when casting but once again, nothing too tricky. If money is no object, perhaps just hire a Ghost.

I have deliberately not gone into too much detail about the Ghost's appearance and often have simply written 'Ghost appears in auditorium' – exactly where or how is left up to you. As for his appearance in a physical sense – let's just say he has to be terrifying.

Happy haunting.

J. C.
September 2015